Do you understand the sadness of geography?
— Michael Ondaatje, *The English Patient*

THE
SADNESS OF
GEOGRAPHY

Logathasan
Tharmathurai

THE
SADNESS OF
GEOGRAPHY

My Life as a Tamil Exile

DUNDURN
TORONTO

Cover image: istock.com/pilesasmiles. All interior images courtesy of the author.
Printer: Webcom, a division of Marquis Book Printing Inc.

Library and Archives Canada Cataloguing in Publication

Title: The sadness of geography : my life as a Tamil exile / Logathasan Tharmathurai.
Names: Tharmathurai, Logathasan, 1966- author.
Identifiers: Canadiana (print) 20190084111 | Canadiana (ebook) 2019008412X | ISBN 9781459745025
   (softcover) | ISBN 9781459745032 (PDF) | ISBN 9781459745049 (EPUB)
Subjects: LCSH: Tharmathurai, Logathasan, 1966- | LCSH: Refugees—Sri Lanka—Biography. |
   LCSH:
   Refugees—Canada—Biography. | LCSH: Tamil (Indic people)—Sri Lanka—Biography. | LCSH:
   Sri Lanka—
   History—Civil War, 1983-2009—Personal narratives, Tamil. | CSH: Tamil Canadians—Biography |
   LCGFT: Autobiographies.
Classification: LCC DS489.86.T43 A3 2019 | DDC 954.9303/2092—dc23

1 2 3 4 5 · 23 22 21 20 19

We acknowledge the support of the Canada Council for the Arts, which last year invested $153 million to bring the arts to Canadians throughout the country, and the Ontario Arts Council for our publishing program. We also acknowledge the financial support of the Government of Ontario, through the Ontario Book Publishing Tax Credit and Ontario Creates, and the Government of Canada.

Nous remercions le Conseil des arts du Canada de son soutien. L'an dernier, le Conseil a investi 153 millions de dollars pour mettre de l'art dans la vie des Canadiennes et des Canadiens de tout le pays.

Care has been taken to trace the ownership of copyright material used in this book. The author and the publisher welcome any information enabling them to rectify any references or credits in subsequent editions.

The publisher is not responsible for websites or their content unless they are owned by the publisher.

Printed and bound in Canada.

VISIT US AT

dundurn.com | @dundurnpress | dundurnpress | dundurnpress

Dundurn
3 Church Street, Suite 500
Toronto, Ontario, Canada
M5E 1M2

To Celia, Eric, and Daniel

PROLOGUE

I sit in the plane at Mirabel Airport in Montreal, gazing out the window at the snow-covered tarmac. I have been travelling under a false name for six months and living as an exile for much longer. It has been more than a year since I left Sri Lanka, my beloved homeland, which is being torn apart by civil war.

I am the last passenger to disembark and the last to join the line at immigration.

Before I left London, my Tamil friends told me that I would have to surrender my illegal passport and declare my true identity to immigration officials at the airport in order to be granted asylum in Canada. It had to be done at the port of entry. If I were to leave the airport with the illegal passport and then try to apply for asylum later, I would be deported back to Sri Lanka.

I am nervous, torn. *Should I declare my true identity or leave the airport as an illegal French national and figure it out later?* I am tired of living as a fugitive, but what if I tell them the truth and they arrest me?

Finally, it is my turn.

At the last moment, I decide to trust my instincts and take the risk. I approach the immigration officer and hand over my illegal passport. "I am Tamil from Sri Lanka and would like to apply for asylum here in Canada," I say.

I am not sure if the officer has heard me. My throat is so dry that I find it hard to speak.

The officer does nothing at first. But finally he stands up from his chair behind the desk and instructs me, with a flick of his hand, to follow him. We enter a small cinder-block office with no windows and just a few chairs. He motions for me to sit down. He leaves, closing the door behind him. I hear it lock.

I am alone.

CHAPTER 1

Sangkaththaanai, Jaffna District, Northern Province, Sri Lanka
1983

"Elumpu! Elumpu!"

E I woke up suddenly, in the dark, startled. *Am I dreaming?*

My father was standing over me, his face bent low to mine. He straightened up, then kicked me, hard. "Elumpu!" *Wake up.*

"I am awake," I answered sleepily, although I wasn't sure why. No lights were on. I could hear smothered whispers as my brothers and sisters moved around hastily in the house.

I begged my father to tell me what was happening.

"Aamykarar vaarangal!" my father whispered. *The army is coming.* "Oodippoi oliyada!" *Run away and hide.*

Groggy with sleep, I rose clumsily but quickly from my bed on the floor.

It was still pitch dark inside the house. I peeked through the window. It was silent. The moon was gone; soon it would be dawn.

"Now!" my father hissed, yanking me along.

When the weather was hot, my brothers and I preferred to sleep on blankets strewn across the concrete floors in the front hall of our house, where it was much cooler. My father, however, had his own room and insisted on sleeping on a cushioned bed under the ceiling fan. My mother, my aunt, and my sisters slept on wooden beds topped with comforters.

I looked for Kanna, my younger brother, but could see only blankets scattered on the floor. Perhaps he was hiding or had run away already.

"Where should I go?" I blurted out, confused. I rubbed my eyes, attempting to bring my father's dark silhouette into focus, but he was just a blur. I could hear more panicked rustling and harsh, muffled whispering from my mother and sisters.

"Be quiet!" my father said. "Go! Run!"

I blundered forward in the dark but slipped on a blanket and tumbled hard to the floor. It seemed easier and faster to crawl. I crawled as quickly as I could to the kitchen, where I found the key to the back door and flung it open. I ran outside, then froze. I turned back momentarily, looking for my two brothers and sisters, hoping they'd followed. I did not like the idea of being on my own.

"Lathy!" I called back into the house, hoping my older brother would appear. "Kanna?"

Where are my brothers? Should I wait?

I squatted in the darkness of our backyard for just a moment, one that seemed like an eternity, wondering what to do.

Where can I run?

I could hear the soft rustling of the wind passing between the leaves on the coconut tree, a soothing hush that belied the terror of the moment. My body felt like ice and my heart was pounding so hard it felt as if it would burst through my chest.

In the distance, a rooster was crowing. With the coming of the sun, the soldiers would appear and I would be caught. I had heard stories of what the soldiers did to Tamil boys. I was just a teenager and I could easily become their prey. They would murder me — or worse.

I could hear another sound: trucks on the main road outside our small village.

"Lathy! Kanna!" I called out again.

Nothing.

I couldn't wait for my brothers; I needed to go.

I stumbled through our backyard garden and crept along the high cement wall at the edge of our property. It was at least seven feet high. Even if I could climb it, the razor-sharp broken bottles anchored to the top — meant to keep intruders out — dissuaded me from even trying.

My mind was racing. Could I risk going through the front gate? There was no place to hide on the road, and I could not outrun the trucks. The soldiers would see me, assume I was a rebel.

I had no choice.

I propped an old piece of discarded lumber against the wall to hoist myself to the top. I had one hand on top of the wall when the piece of wood snapped. I crashed to the ground.

"Ennada saniyan!" I swore.

I jumped to my feet and circled the yard in a panic. There was nothing else to help me scale the wall.

I willed my heart to stop thumping long enough for me to listen. I could hear the trucks coming closer: the deep-throated sound of shifting gears, the revving of the engines, the shrieking of brakes.

By this time, the stingy early morning light was bringing the flat contours of our backyard into relief. I felt unbearably exposed.

I'm trapped!

I had no choice but to use the front gate. If there was a soldier on the road, however, there would be nowhere for me to hide. My knees trembled; suddenly I felt a warm dribble on my leg. I felt my sarong with my hand, ashamed to discover that I'd wet myself. How Lathy would make fun of me if he knew! In my shame, thinking of how he would tease me was almost as bad as my fear of the soldiers.

All I wanted to do was disappear, but somehow I convinced myself to creep around the side of the house. Our front gate was made of iron bars. In fact, it was the *only* iron gate in the neighbourhood. Most of the families in our neighbourhood were too poor to afford iron gates, which is probably why my father had insisted on having one. In our village, fences were usually woven from coconut leaves and affixed at intervals to the trees that lined the street. My father was a proud, prosperous, and well-respected businessman; exhibiting and maintaining his status was very important to him. He insisted the gate be locked every night against intruders. After all, the driveway was wide enough for two cars — even though we never had two cars. Most families in the village didn't have even one car. The majority had bicycles or scooters, or simply walked.

In any case, the gate was no obstacle. I was barefoot, which made climbing it easier.

At the top, I looked up and down the road but did not see any soldiers or military trucks. I jumped.

The road in front of our house, like all the roads in our village, was unpaved. Luckily my feet were tough from walking barefoot; otherwise, landing on the sharp stones would have been painful. Even so, I winced and hopped before starting to run.

I stayed low, sticking as close to the side of the road as I could to remain inconspicuous. After just a few steps, I skidded to a halt. A military truck had stopped at the top of the road. Soldiers dressed in green and brown camouflage and carrying submachine guns were jumping from the back of the truck and fanning out in groups of three or four along the road. At each house, a group of soldiers would duck into the laneway.

Except for the faint crunching of boots on the gravel, the soldiers were eerily quiet, like ghosts. Suddenly the silence was broken by shouting, first in one house and then another, and another, like slowly toppling dominoes. Orders were being barked. Rough male voices, then women's screams and wails.

Get off the road!

I ran into my neighbour's yard. Unlike our large, modern house, many homes in the village were crude and very small — several of them no more than improvised shacks or huts. Most had a tiny porch at the front and one big sleeping room for the family. The kitchen was cramped and had firepits made of clay for cooking. Toilets were located at the back, separate from the house. Some houses had a well, but none, except ours, had running water. Anyone who could manage it had a modest garden to grow vegetables and some little cages in which to raise chickens.

The shouts from the soldiers grew louder as they got closer. From the houses I could hear the shrill, terrified cries of women and girls. I zigzagged from one backyard to another until I reached a railway crossing. From behind some bushes I could see military trucks driving along the main road, known as the Kandy–Jaffna Highway. Soldiers were moving from house to house, searching. My only hope was to reach the rice paddies beyond the highway. Our house was only a short distance from the highway; the fields, however, were about four miles away, and I had no way of knowing if I could make it that far without being seen.

What if soldiers had been stationed at the fields to watch for boys and men making a run for it?

I waited by the highway, hiding behind the bushes until a short convoy of military trucks had passed. Then, crouching low, I ran as fast as I could across the tar-paved road toward the Sangkaththaanai Kanthasamy Kovil, a Hindu temple in our village. Years later, I can still recall the soft sound of my bare feet slapping the tar road as I ran.

I passed the temple and kept running, away from home, toward the paddies. The fields at the edge of the paddies were lined with mature trees with enough foliage to help obscure my movements.

I was panting, breathless, and slowed down to catch my breath. *What a beautiful morning*, I caught myself thinking, as if in a dream. I would never forget the image of the fiery edge of sunrise in the distance and the blue sky arcing above the green rice fields.

Just as suddenly as before, more trucks appeared nearby and my sense of security instantly disappeared. I hurried down a narrow path that split the rice paddy into two sections and was soon surrounded by rice stalks — bright green at that time of year — that reached to my shoulders. It was midseason, and the ground was still wet and muddy from a heavy rainfall the night before. It was early, but the sun would soon be a torch in the sky. I was alone. I had no idea what was happening to my family. There was nothing I could do but hide. And wait.

The rice paddy was strangely peaceful. The contrast was overwhelming and deeply disorienting. As frightened as I was, the coiled tightness in my chest began to ease, like ice melting. My heartbeat slowed to something more like normal. *I am probably safe for now*, I thought. I figured it was unlikely the soldiers would enter open ground in pursuit of Tamil guerillas — especially in my village, an area of northern Sri Lanka known for being sympathetic to the guerillas. It was said by many Sinhalese that a favourite tactic of the Tamil guerillas was luring soldiers into ambushes.

It had only been a few months since the terrible eruption of the Black July attacks and violence against Tamils, and tensions between Tamils and Sinhalese were at their peak. The majority Sinhalese government was cracking down hard on the minority Tamil population for alleged attacks by armed guerillas. Most Tamils were not guerillas; all Tamils, however, were under suspicion, especially young men and boys. It was well known that teenage Tamil boys — boys like me — were eagerly recruited by the guerillas.

It is true. I should know. I would eventually be recruited, too.

All my life I had lived exclusively among Tamils. Of course, I had seen Sinhalese now and again but had never had any real contact with them. I used to wonder what they were like; I wondered, too, why they hated the Tamils. How can you hate someone so much even though you have never met them?

In the previous few months, we'd begun seeing Sinhalese soldiers all the time. They never smiled; they obviously hated us, and they treated us as if we were less than animals. There was nothing we could do. So why not join the rebels? The rebels wanted respect for the Tamil people. They promised the Tamils that we would be treated fairly and with justice. The Tamil people had been in Sri Lanka for centuries — at least since the second century BCE — but we were treated by the Sinhalese as if we did not belong, as if we had no roots in the country, as if it were not just as much our home as theirs. They claimed that we only stole and begged, that we had made no contribution to the country.

As I walked through the field, I could not stop thinking about what might be happening at home. About what they were doing to my father and brothers, to my mother and sisters.

All of a sudden, I heard an unfamiliar sound in the distance. It was a sort of *whomp-whomp* sound, weak at first but getting louder and louder. I searched the sky, and in the bright early morning sunlight something appeared as a glowing silver bullet, moving very fast but low — and coming directly at me.

A military helicopter!

I started to run. The rice plants were tall and green and the sprouts were yellow, and as I brushed past them they reminded me of tiny bells attached to a long stick. As I ran deeper into the field, my feet began to disappear into the muddy ground; each step became harder and harder as I sank deeper and deeper into the mud. I knocked aside the tiny bells as the *whomp-whomp* approached, closer and closer. As the helicopter swooped overhead, I dropped face down into the mud.

The helicopter was flying low enough that I could feel the thumping of the blades like punches to my body. I dug myself into the mud, but it wasn't deep enough. I wallowed in the earth, twisting and turning, slathering myself in mud, trying to sink in farther.

The helicopter swung around for another pass and I lay still as death. Between each pass, I tried to dig myself deeper and deeper into the mud, to obliterate myself. With each pass, the thumping blades created powerful gusts of wind that sent the tiny bells into a chiming frenzy.

I lay face down in the mud for what felt like hours, my heart pounding so loud it almost overpowered the deafening *whomp-whomp* of the helicopter.

They will find me. They will kill me.

I was crying, but the tears dissolved harmlessly in the mud. I wondered if I would ever see my family again, about what would happen to me if I got caught. How would my mother feel if I didn't return home? I worried about my brothers. Where had they gone? Were they safe?

As suddenly as the helicopter had appeared, it disappeared, like the sun moving behind a bank of clouds. I didn't dare move, however, and for hours I lay in the mud, feeling the scorching heat of the sun on my back. It was hard to move. My legs and arms were stiffly encased in the baking mud, but the rice plants were cool. I was desperately thirsty, but the water I managed to lap up was mixed with mud and had an unpleasant mineral sharpness in my mouth and on my tongue.

All that morning and afternoon no one came to the field. There was no sound but the chirring of insects in the tall plants, the sucking noise of the embracive mud as I tried to move my aching limbs, the occasional faraway sound of traffic on the road. I waited in dread-filled silence.

Hours later — I think; I have no idea how long I lay there — I heard the fast-approaching *whomp-whomp* of another helicopter. My heart sank. It roared overhead and into the distance, only to return a short time later from the other direction. It happened again not long after. And again.

The soldiers must know a boy is missing from the village. They are searching for me. They must know I am in the fields.

I was torn between running again and remaining in the field. I convinced myself the soldiers were waiting for me. Waiting to catch me. I kept waiting.

I was very hungry and badly needed to pee. Too afraid to risk standing up — or even moving more than an inch or two — I stayed where I was hiding and urinated. It wasn't so embarrassing this time; it actually felt good. I was so tense and tight it was a relief to let go and feel my body flushing itself, purging. Almost immediately, however, the pleasing sensation disappeared. I smelled horrible.

I could feel the sun moving lower on the horizon. My legs were numb. My stomach was rumbling from hunger. All I could think about, however, were the soldiers on the road and in the village.

Deliberately, slowly, I uprooted myself from the mud and turned to stare up at the sky. It had shifted from bright blue to dark blue and orange. It would be dark soon. It had been quite a while since I had heard the helicopter. It was time.

When I attempted to stand up, my legs felt as stiff as boards and I stumbled. The wet mud had hardened on my back and on my legs and shoulders. I could feel my shirt crack as I stretched. I must have looked like a zombie. My hair felt like stiff straw and my head itched.

The sky was empty and serene. I walked to the dirt path that led to the road. I noticed deep ruts — from heavy wheels and tread marks — in the soft ground; there were booted footprints, too, that trailed off in various directions. Had the helicopter spotted me? Had the soldiers waited for me, perhaps fearing that I was a rebel lying in wait to ambush them if they approached?

I stumbled across the tar road, careful to keep watch around me just in case, and headed back to the village. I couldn't see any military trucks anywhere. Past the temple along the road to our house I heard moaning noises coming from one house. Farther along, I passed by another house and heard more sad wailing. As I walked along the road I saw mothers sitting on the ground, smacking their heads, rocking and sobbing.

"Aiyoo, amma!" they chanted. *Oh, my mother!* It was a familiar lament in Tamil, a common expression of deep sadness. *Aiyoo* is an exclamatory term used in spoken Tamil when something terrible happens to someone, when someone feels sorry for something that has happened; it is also uttered when someone witnesses something frightening.

"Aen entai pillaiai kondu pottai?" *Why did you take my child?*

"Eppa naan entai pillaiai pakka poran? Kadavulai, engalai kappathtu." *When am I going to see my child again? Lord, protect us.*

Occasionally I heard screaming: brief bursts, like choking sobs, or long and drawn out like a mournful wind. The mothers were bewailing their sons' abductions.

It is a tradition in Hindu culture, even among the poor, to wear fresh clothes every day — a sarong for the men and a sari for the women. In our village, women always wear fresh flowers in their hair. Men ritually adorn their forehead with a streak of powder known as thiruneeru, a sacred ash used in religious worship in Hinduism. Women wear the pottu on their foreheads, the familiar red dot, which usually signifies their status as married women but is sometimes worn as an omen to ward off evil.

In the late afternoon, most people in the village would have been on their way to or from temple. But not that day. The men and women I saw in the streets looked haggard and rumpled, dishevelled even. None of the men wore the thiruneeru or the women the pottu. Oddly, despite everything I had seen and experienced that day, it was the unexpected unkemptness of the men and women I encountered on the roads that frightened me the most.

As I reached the end of our road, I could see my father and mother standing by the gate of our home.

"Amma!" I shouted in greeting.

They looked terrified. They must not have recognized me. Bursting into tears, I ran to my mother. "Amma!" I sobbed.

Once they realized that it was me, their faces lit up with happiness. My mother wrapped her arms around me in a big hug. "Rajan, my son! Where have you been?" Rajan is my Tamil nickname. Her tone was anguished but scolding as she hugged me tight. "Where were you? We were so worried the army took you from us." She would not relax her arms. I thought I might suffocate.

"Amma," I said, "you're squeezing me to death!"

Only then did she relax. She was smiling, but tears streaked her face.

My father was a man who never expressed his emotions — at least not with me — and when he saw that I was safe, he simply nodded and turned to go back inside the house. I asked my mother about my brothers and sisters: Lathy, Kanna, Deicy, Jance, Vani, and Kala.

"Kanna was hiding in the chimney," she told me. "Lucky for us the soldiers arrived before breakfast!" My older brother, Lathy, she said, had run away to our grandmother's house a couple of blocks away. "I suppose the soldiers assumed that an old woman living alone in a small house had no family," my mother explained. "Or maybe she was not worth bothering about. Your sisters are unharmed. They are safe."

She led me to the house, but at the front door she stopped, looked at me, and pinched her nose in disgust. "Rajan, you must wash immediately. You stink!"

I burst out laughing and did as she said.

After showering and changing into clean clothes, I was suddenly overcome with fatigue. For supper my mother had prepared sweet roti, my favourite. We did not talk about what had happened, and after dinner we all went to bed. As tired as I was, I did not sleep.

CHAPTER 2

In the days that followed the raid, I would learn that many boys from my village were missing. Families with sons who had been captured by the soldiers were confronted by a wall of bureaucratic silence when they attempted to track them down. The military authorities would not even admit to having raided the village, much less acknowledge stealing innocent young men at gunpoint at the crack of dawn. And if a boy had been taken and a reason had to be provided, the explanation was simple: *He was a member of a guerilla group responsible for the murder of innocent civilians.* After a time, the families just gave up. It was safer that way.

It was not uncommon, either, for captured young Tamil men to be sent by the army to the military garrison Poonakari, in the Northern Province, for detention or torture. In order to understand the Tamil sense of nationalism and its experience with self-exile, history helps underscore the irony of this: Poonakari was built by the colonizing Portuguese in the eighteenth century to "protect its possessions." It was later expanded by the conquering Dutch to do the same. The British, in turn, took it over and held it until Sri Lanka gained independence in 1948. After the outbreak of civil war in 1983, the Sri Lankan Army established a garrison at Poonakari to put down the Tamils.

Either way, whether a family's son had just vanished or had been sent to Poonakari, he was lost.

A lot of young boys and men disappeared from our village that day. Some of them were captured by the Sri Lankan soldiers and others joined the guerilla groups. One of my cousins, Manikanna, was captured. I never heard from him again.

It was the most terrifying day of my life. In many ways, the happy life I had known ended that day.

The effects of the raid on the other people in the village were plainly evident, too. Everyone was afraid to leave their homes. Parents continued to bemoan the loss of their children. People who used to go to the temple early in the morning, before their daily chores, stopped going. The temple bells in our village ceased ringing. Buses stopped running. Schools were shut down frequently. Our famous Chavakachcheri market was left deserted. Shops were closed.

My father did not discuss this with us, but I know it troubled him. He hated being forced to stay at home, doing nothing. He became restless and started drinking in the mornings.

Curfews were put in place randomly. The Sri Lankan military started to penetrate our villages and towns. Initially, we would see three or four trucks, but within a month of the raid, I began to see not only many trucks full of soldiers but also armoured vehicles with machine guns mounted on the top. The military forces were building up in the Tamil-occupied areas.

Nothing would ever be the same.

I had to leave.

CHAPTER 3

[S]ome men are born out of their due place. Accident has
cast them amid certain surroundings, but they have always a
nostalgia for a home they know not. They are strangers in their
birthplace.... They may spend their whole lives aliens among
their kindred and remain aloof among the only scenes they
have ever known.
— W. Somerset Maugham, *The Moon and Sixpence*

Sri Lanka is a beautiful, mango-shaped island in the
Indian Ocean. I have heard it described as pear-shaped,
which, for the literal-minded, is probably more accu-
rate. For me, however, and for many Sri Lankans, our nation
has the shape of our favourite fruit, the mango. And so it does.

When I was growing up in Sri Lanka, I thought it was the only place on Earth. I am proud to have called Sri Lanka home. The country is blessed with diverse landscapes: rainforest and dry plains, highlands and gorgeous sun-drenched sandy beaches. The colour of the ocean is like no other in the world — more like a shimmering jewel than a colour. As a boy, nothing was more beautiful to me. I still recall with fondness the abundance of beaches, forests, temples, forts, historical sites, and magnificent birds and animals.

I grew up in Sangkaththaanai, a small village in the Jaffna District of the Northern Province. A short distance away was a larger town, Chavakachcheri, known as the second-largest business hub in the Northern Province (Jaffna being the largest). People from other cities, towns, and villages in the province came to Chavakachcheri to trade. It was where my father had his jewellery shop.

Every Friday when I was a child, my father would take us to Jaffna Muneeswaran Temple, a Hindu place of worship located adjacent to Jaffna Fort. When I was a little boy, my mother often sent us off to sleep with bedtime stories, and one I enjoyed in particular was the story of the fort. According to my mother, the fort was built in Jaffna by the Portuguese in 1618, following their invasion. Later, in 1658, the Dutch captured and then expanded it. The British took control of it in 1795, and it remained under British control until 1948. More than the history lessons, though, I enjoyed my mother's ghoulish tales as we walked past the fort about the prisoners who were kept inside. I would shiver when she pointed out the tower where the prisoners were hanged in the old days.

My siblings and I loved to go to the temple with my father but not necessarily to worship. My younger brother, Kanna, and I loved to run and play around the grounds. But what my brothers and I enjoyed most was watching the horses parading in and out of the adjacent fort. More than half of the fort was surrounded by swampland; later, when I saw pictures of Alcatraz, the island prison off San Francisco, I felt a sense of déjà vu.

After a Friday temple visit, my father would take us to a fancy restaurant for dinner and then to the ice-cream café for dessert. My father generally ate first — and my mother would stand next to him and serve the rest of his meals. After he finished eating, my mother would serve my siblings and me dinner. Only after we had eaten would my mother eat. Thus, Friday nights at the fancy restaurants in Jaffna were the only time we ever really ate as a family.

Subhas ice-cream café was one of the best and busiest in the city of Jaffna. The ice-cream bar had air conditioning — an enchanting luxury in those days — and was illuminated with eerie blue neon lights that cast an otherworldly glow over the patrons. It felt to me like an ice palace.

I always ordered a sundae that had nuts on the bottom, then ice cream in the middle and jelly on top. After dessert, my father would take us all to watch movies. Because he was a prosperous businessman, he could afford a private booth at the cinema with butler service, and the butler would bring us an unlimited amount of chocolates, peanuts, and sodas. It didn't matter how much ice cream I had eaten for dessert; there was always more room for Kandos chocolates at the cinema.

Although my siblings and I looked forward to these Friday evenings, we had to be careful not to say the wrong thing to my father. It was the only time we ate together, but out of respect we didn't say a word as we ate.

CHAPTER 4

By serving the father with regularity, one may cross this world.
By serving the mother in the same way, one may attain to
regions of felicity in the next. By serving the preceptor with
regularity one may obtain the region of Brahma. Behave properly towards these three, O Bharata, you will then obtain great
fame in the three worlds, and you will be blessed, great will
be your merit and reward.

— The Mahabharata

My father, Tharmathurai Rasiah (in Tamil culture, the family takes the father's first name as their last name), was born in Sangkaththaanai, too, as was his father. Most of my father's large extended family lived there as well.

When I was growing up, our house was by far the largest and most modern in Sangkaththaanai. My father was very proud of that and always made sure he was the first to have any modern convenience. We were the first to have running water and the first to have electricity. My father bought the first automobile in the village.

When mail was sent to our house, it was not necessary to put a number and street name on the envelope, or even the name of the village; it would simply read *Tharmathurai Rasiah, Chavakachcheri*. Everyone from miles around knew who my father was.

There could not have been more than three hundred families living in Sangkaththaanai back then, and a large number of those were of my father's clan. Other houses tended to be built around ours. The poorest houses — hardly more than huts — were home to the lower-caste villagers — fishermen, farmers, and common labourers — with whom we did not associate. I remember as a child playing with my cousins from my father's family; I do not remember playing much with the village children.

Of course, in a big city we would have been looked down upon, but in Sangkaththaanai, my father was like a king, and we lived in conspicuous luxury.

It was my grandfather who had started the jewellery business, and as the eldest son, it was my father who took it over. The shop my father managed in Chavakachcheri had been built by my grandfather. It was larger than the other jewellery shops in town, and under my father's management, it was enormously profitable.

My father did not have much in the way of a formal education, but he had a gift for numbers and bookkeeping. He was also strict and suspicious that workers in his employ were cheating him. It was a common gambit for wholesale gold to be mixed with copper, so he was always scrupulous when it came to judging the jewellery delivered to the shop.

Besides being rich, my father was a very handsome man — light skinned with jet-black hair and brown eyes — and was considered a most enviable match. He was also extremely fastidious about his appearance. I suppose it had a lot to do with his success. Every day, he shaved and combed his hair neatly, and he never left the house without attending to his clothes. He always dressed the part of the successful businessman.

Studio photo of Aiya (Father) taken in Chavakachcheri when he was around thirty-five years old.

Most days after closing up the shop, my father would meet up with his friends and business colleagues at an upscale bar in town. He was respected and well liked in our town, and he was known for being generous when it came to hospitality. In other words, he liked to stand his friends free drinks.

As far as I know, he never asked my mother to accompany him on his forays into town. Every now and again they might go to the movies. My father liked showing her off, I think, at fancy restaurants. But he also had a roving eye when it came to women.

I came to understand that my father was — besides handsome and successful — a charming and fun-loving man. He also had, I was to learn, a selfish understanding of what was fun. But I remember him mostly as a rather stern and impatient father who was not much amused by the antics of small boys. He never played with us or seemed interested in anything we were up to.

In Tamil culture, only the elders are allowed to initiate a conversation. Because of this, we rarely talked to our father; we only replied when spoken to. My father did not often ask my opinion on any topic. My father was always — and remains — an enigma to me.

I do vividly remember following my father around when we visited stores. He was so proud of his success that he refused to check the price of items. He liked to carry a big bundle of cash in his pocket, and if he saw something he liked, he would say, "I want that." The vendors, of course, knew that he was rich and often jacked up the price. My father did not care. In fact, I think he was flattered. It was a sign of his stature. He would casually hand over a stack of bills, making sure the vendor and anyone watching understood he was overpaying — often lavishly. The vendor would bow and grovel in an ostentatious display of gratitude and my father would nod regally and walk on. He never asked for change.

One day I had a bright idea. Tagging closely behind my father — everyone knew I was his son — I hung back just long enough to demand the change from the vendor. What could he do? I pocketed the change and caught up with my father at the next stall. My father never discovered my ruse, but the vendors were not happy at all!

I cannot say that I really ever knew my father in any meaningful sense. He took his success very seriously and I think he loved us in the dutiful, almost obligatory way that some fathers love their children. He wasn't mean or aggressive with us; quite the opposite. He would do whatever he needed to do to protect us, to help us succeed in whatever path we chose, but that was as far as it went. He was unfailingly generous, but he had no capacity for intimacy, at least not with children. He treated his family as he managed his business. He wanted us to be successful, and he did his best to provide. To me, however, he was a cold and distant satellite in my emotional universe.

CHAPTER 5

For women there is no ornament more
valuable than their husbands.
— Valmiki Ramayana Sundara Kanda

My mother, Yogambal Tharmathurai, came from a small farming village called Mulliyawalai, about sixty miles inland from Sangkaththaanai. In those days, that was a very long way away.

Her father worked on a modest farm. I remember my grandfather as an incredibly hard-working man who was in the fields by five in the morning and rarely returned home before the sun went down. He was kind, too, and was always very good to me. He shaved infrequently and I can still recall the feeling of his sharp whiskers on my face as he greeted me with a kiss when I visited him.

When my parents married, my mother left her hometown to move in with my father in Sangkaththaanai. It must have been difficult leaving her family behind and suddenly living among a brand-new family she did not know.

In the photographs I have seen of my mother as a young woman — she was about eighteen when she was married — she was beautiful. She had big eyes and long, lustrous hair, and when I was a child she wore colourful saris and lots of jewellery. Every morning, she would put the red pottu on her forehead as well as the traditional thali necklace. "It means I am married to your father," she told me.

The thali she devotedly wore had been fastened around her neck by my father on their wedding day. My mother loved my father deeply; she was also a devoted Hindu who took her role as wife and mother very seriously. She disciplined us and made sure that we respected not only my father but also my older brother, Lathy. The eldest son was next in line to the father in terms of deserving respect. It was the eldest son who would inherit the family business; not only that, he would inherit all the responsibilities and obligations that came with being head of the family.

In Hindu culture, a wife is absolutely required to remain faithful to her husband, no matter what. There is a passage in the great Hindu holy text the Mahabharata that reads, "Women have one eternal duty in this world, viz., dependence upon and obedient service to their husbands, and as such, this one duty constitutes their only end." It is an extremely difficult passage to read today, especially for us in the West, but Hindu women of that time in Sri Lanka — women like my

Wedding photo of Aiya (Father) and Amma (Mother), 1963.

mother — took their traditional obligations seriously. I must admit I have had a very hard time coming to terms with her commitment to my father, especially now, as a father myself to children who thrive in a completely different environment.

Early one morning when I was six years old, I was sleeping on a mat on the floor, as usual. I was awakened by a young woman, around seventeen years old, sweeping the cement floor next to me. I opened my eyes, confused, and stared at her, wondering what she was doing in our home. Immediately, I got up and went to look for my mother.

"Who is she?" I asked.

"She is my sister," Mother replied.

"What is she doing here?"

"She came with your father last night," she replied. I noticed she had tears in her eyes.

I had no idea what was going on. I was too young to understand. But slowly, as the days went by, I realized my aunt was now living with us. My father never mentioned her or explained why she was at our house, but he doted on her and seemed overly friendly. I would hear them whispering together late at night, and my aunt would often stay with my father in his bedroom.

At the same time, my father seemed to drift away from my mother. Often, they would not speak for weeks.

My father would take my aunt out with him in the evening but not my mother. He owned a shiny white Peugeot 404, and he liked to drive my aunt to the movies and Lions Club parties. She was much younger than my mother, and I suspect my father enjoyed showing off his new trophy mistress. For formality's sake, he would take my mother to the temple, weddings, and other local events. But when it came time for fun, it was always my aunt he spent time with. My father was living two separate lives.

Deep down, I harboured a heavy resentment toward my father because of his amorous relationship with my aunt. This hatred was strongest whenever he bought new saris or jewellery. He would always let my aunt choose what she wanted before giving the leftovers to my mother.

"I am okay. Your father will get mad if he hears you," my mother assured me when I questioned her the first time this happened.

To this day, I do not understand my mother's willingness to forgive both her husband and her sister.

My father had grown up as the eldest son of eleven — six brothers and five sisters — for whose welfare he became responsible. He was relatively young when his father gave his shop to him and built the second shop for himself in another town. My father stopped going to school and began working full-time. I don't know if my father had ever had dreams of his own or how he felt about having to leave school; he never spoke to me about it. I suspect that, like many boys of his generation, he simply obeyed his father and put his own wishes to the side.

When I was a child, my father employed an accountant, Kidduswamy, and one of my father's brothers-in-law, Santhiran, to run errands at the store and perform odd jobs. At the back of the store, my father built small quarters for about six workers, who lived there and made jewellery. Hanny, our chauffeur, drove my father to the shop most mornings, but sometimes he would ride his bike to work. Occasionally, Hanny also drove us to school in Jaffna, as well as to stores and on assorted errands.

In the mornings, I would help to open the store and get everything ready for my father. I would sweep the floors, tidy up, wash the main entrance, light the incense, and spray the ritual holy water throughout the store. Next, I'd walk to a local tuck shop to buy dosai, a type of pancake made from fermented batter, to feed to the crows, which was supposed to bring good luck to the store. Not long after that, my father would appear, and I would walk or bike home to get ready for school. Before my older brother, Lathy, went away to boarding school, this had been his job. I had the job for about two years before I also went off to boarding school, after which Kanna took over.

It was my father's responsibility not only to pay dowries for his sisters when they were married but also to have houses built for them in our village. He also employed his brothers-in-law at the jewellery shop. He brought electricity to our village and helped to build Sri Meenakshi Amman Kovil, a temple in Sangkaththaanai. My father was a hero in our village, and no one had the courage to speak against him.

I can only wonder what this all meant for my mother. She had left her family when she married my father and came to live with him in his village, surrounded by *his* family. She never complained, but even if she had wanted to talk with someone, it would have been difficult. Whom could she trust? The only people she knew were her husband's relatives, and they would never allow a bad word to be said against him.

In Tamil culture, once a woman marries, she leaves her parents and moves in with her husband for life. I'd never heard of a divorce or separation in my village.

One day, on my way home from school, I noticed a crowd of people gathered around the well outside our home. They were yelling and screaming, and a rope was being lowered frantically into the well. I ran up to the well and peeked in. It was about fifty feet deep and very dark.

"What is happening?" I asked, but no one paid any attention to me. Suddenly, out of the darkness of the well, a figure emerged, illuminated by a beam of sunlight.

"Amma!" I screamed. My mother's face, hollow and sad, stared up at me. She saw me crying.

"Amma," I blubbered. "Please come up. I need you!" I was sobbing and screaming for her to come out of the well. Someone pulled me back and tried to comfort me, but I was hysterical.

When my mother was pulled from the well a few minutes later, I broke away, ran to her, and threw myself into her arms. I hugged her tightly and could not stop crying.

Not a word about the incident was ever spoken, and it was only many years later that I asked my mother about it. Even then, she was reluctant to discuss it in detail. She said only that she and my father had had an argument. At one point she threatened to jump into the well. He was so mad that he threw up his hands in defeat and said, "Fine! Jump in the well!" So she did.

Luckily, it was the dry season. The well water was deep enough to break her fall but not deep enough to drown her.

I am not sure my father had believed she would actually have the nerve to jump. Upset, he ran to the neighbours for help. In the panicked scene, I remember him only vaguely, hovering in the background, looking angry and embarrassed.

A few weeks later, my father added an extension to our home, which, besides creating a separate living space for my mother, included a separate bedroom for my aunt. What that really meant, however, was a room for him and my aunt. In a sense, he had two wives from that point. No one — family or friends — approved of the arrangement, and it was only because my father was such a powerful and respected man that it was tolerated.

This was before the outbreak of civil war in Sri Lanka, when my father was doing very well and business was booming.

As I said, my father was an attractive man, and young women flooded the jewellery shop. In fact, while he was with my mother and aunt, he had another affair with a young teacher. She would often visit the shop in the evening, and my father would send me away on errands while she was there. One day, the woman visited our home, and my aunt, jealous with rage, threw all our marble plates on the floor and broke the windows in the bedroom. As usual, my mother remained very quiet. After that, however, my father never brought the teacher home. Apparently, he ended up meeting her secretly at her home for a while.

Our family no longer ate together, even on Fridays. My mother and my aunt would cook separately in their own kitchens. When my father came home to eat, he would take his meal with my aunt.

A year later, my aunt gave birth to a baby girl: my half-sister, Kala. We all adored her. Eventually, Kala ended up spending more time with my mother than with her own, and my aunt resented the relationship. "I am your mother!" she would yell at Kala. "You call *me* Amma!" My aunt had a bad temper; in many ways she was hardly more than a child herself.

Whenever this happened, my brother Kanna, my mother, or I would intervene. Kala would call my brothers and me "Anna," which means elder brother. Our love for Kala became stronger, and we grew up together as one family. I cannot begin to imagine how difficult and heartbreaking this situation was for my mother.

With time, I came to understand that it could not have been easy on my aunt either. I discovered later that my father began his affair with my aunt when he and my mother had visited my mother's family. He had been writing intimate letters to her at school when she was only sixteen.

My aunt was probably flattered by my father's attentions. After all, he was a great and respected man! If he was initiating this, then it must be okay. I think she was attracted to my father for other reasons, too; he was charming and dashing and could buy her nice things. But she was not my father's wife. And when she took up with my father, it destroyed her own father, my grandfather, and she was no longer welcome at his house. She lost her family. And she had no real standing with my father's people. It must have been uncomfortable for her, being in the same house with my mother, knowing she was resented and had nowhere else to go.

My aunt rarely left the house on her own. I think she was afraid of what people would say. When she went out, it was always with my father. At home she mostly kept to herself. Sometimes I would hear her and my mother arguing. It was my mother's house, after all.

I resented how much attention my father lavished on my aunt and would find as many opportunities as I could to fight with her. I used to carry a small knife with me and I cut up her clothes, sofa, favourite chairs — anything that I could find to vent my anger on. I was caught a couple of times and my father beat me. My mother scolded me, too, but I am not so sure her heart was in it.

"Amma," I asked her once, "I don't know how you live like this. Why don't you go and live with Grandpa and Grandma?"

"If I leave your father, no one will take care of you and your brothers and sisters. Grandpa and Grandma will be mad at me if I go back."

"But —"

She stopped me cold. "I am living for my children now. I still love your father."

I never discussed this with her again.

My aunt eventually had three daughters with my father: Kala, Sumathi, and Sharmilee. My mother gave birth to two more daughters of her own, Jance and Vani. In time, I stopped questioning our arrangement. Life moved on. What good would asking questions do? Nothing would change.

CHAPTER 6

Though destitute of virtue, or seeking pleasure (elsewhere), or devoid of good qualities, (yet) a husband must be constantly worshipped as a god by a faithful wife.

— The Manusmriti

Not long after the official start of the Sri Lankan civil war, a smaller but hardly less violent civil war had broken out in our home. My uncles and aunts, who lived next door, became convinced that a curse had been placed on my father.

According to my mother, my father had a dream in which the goddess Sri Meenakshi Amman appeared to him, telling him that a woman would visit him to help him with "his problems."

My father's business was failing at the time, and I assume this was the problem that most concerned him. However, his taking as his mistress the younger sister of my mother was taboo in Hindu culture, and my mother's family was incensed. But he was still a powerful and influential man, so what could be done? This unorthodox arrangement did not seem to be a problem in my father's mind; he had been extremely generous with his wife's family, and for that reason, I think he believed he was allowed this indiscretion.

At this point, my mother, father, and aunt had been feuding continually for months. My father had begun drinking heavily as well, and he often came home stumbling drunk and angry. Sometimes he would fight with my mother, sometimes with my aunt, sometimes with both. He would smash furniture, and my uncles and aunts from next door would show up and attempt to calm him down. "You have lost your senses!" they would say. "You are possessed by pey [a demon]. This is not you!"

The evening after his dream, an old woman appeared unannounced at our door. She was what is known in Tamil as a pey turattuvar, a demon chaser. My father strongly believed that this woman was the one prophesied by the goddess in his dream. She came from another village and she performed Hindu rituals in the way of an itinerant preacher. She was a pure Hindu who ate neither meat nor fish and had dedicated herself entirely to devotion to God.

She was invited in and brought to the prayer room in our house. There, she laid out neem leaves (a type of leaf to chase away evil spirits), banana leaves, rice, coconut, limes, holy water, and other odds and ends. She arranged the items on the banana leaves in front of a picture of Kali. Kali is the Hindu goddess of death, time, and doomsday, and is often associated with sexuality and violence, but she is also considered a strong mother figure and is symbolic of motherly love.

My father, mother, Kanna, Lathy, and I were sitting around her as she started the prayer. All the lights were off except for a small kerosene lamp on the floor. Within minutes she became extremely agitated and began talking to herself in incomprehensible words. She swayed her head back and forth, and her body buckled and writhed and rocked from side to side. She was holding my father's hand and repeatedly beating him with the neem leaves. The woman's eyes suddenly rolled up — she stared at us with eyes like shiny white porcelain — and she moaned as if in terrible agony.

All of a sudden, she grabbed one of the limes covered with yellow and red paste, called santhanam and kungumam, respectively. The santhanam is from the sandalwood tree, used in the form of paste in temples. The kungumam is a powder used for social and religious markings, made from turmeric powder and lime. All at once, she sprang to her feet and bounded outside into the front yard. It was very dark out, and my father ran after her carrying the kerosene lamp. Mother, Kanna, Lathy, and I followed. I was terrified. The woman crept along the sand like a spectre, a shadow among shadows, tiptoeing and twitching her arms and legs oddly like a zombie. All of a sudden, she flung the lime into the darkness. Then she froze and lifted her hands, palms out, as if caressing the darkness. She pointed to where the lime had come to rest.

"Dig!" she commanded.

My father began to dig.

He unearthed a metal box. We all gasped. The small box was made of copper, and inside it had been hidden sand, lemon seeds, and lengths of human hair. Human hair was a common ingredient in curses and was associated with many discomforts and maladies. My father handed the box to the woman, and she led us back to the prayer room to resume the ritual.

She put the box down, then suddenly collapsed to the floor and began twitching and jerking and rolling her eyes. "Leave this body!" she commanded. She started shrieking and jerked like she was being stabbed by sharp needles. She rose to her knees, white foam bubbling out of her mouth.

Kanna, Lathy, and I panicked and dashed out of the prayer room and into another room to hide. My parents waited for the old woman to regain consciousness, but she did not. Alarmed that she might have taken ill, they took the old woman to the hospital. The next day, my mother told us, the lady died in her arms at the hospital. She had traded her soul for my father.

My mother claimed that this event had a huge impact on her. After that, no matter what my father ever did, no matter how mean or cruel or selfish he was, her love and devotion to him never wavered.

I have no idea who put the curse on my father. It could have been a member of my father's or my mother's family. I was young, and it is easy to believe anything when one is young. All I know is that my mother believed, and she felt sorry for him. She believed that he had been cursed and he needed help.

It took me a lot longer to feel the same way about my father.

* * *

48

A few years later, my aunt finally reached a breaking point in her relationship with my father. After a bad fight, she moved back to her parents' home with Sumathi and Sharmilee. Kala stayed and lived with us, and my mother continued to treat her as if she were her own daughter. By that time my father was a broken man in both his business and family life. But my mother remained devoted to him.

To this day my mother refuses to discuss her relationship with my father or her sister. I know from my own experience that she is an immensely proud and strong woman. She had to be, to stay with my father all that time and under those conditions.

I don't understand her, but I deeply respect and admire her strength. Whoever I am today, I owe to her — to her love and her incredible strength and her quiet courage.

CHAPTER 7

My older brother, Lathy, was responsible for all his siblings. I often resented his lord-of-the-manor ways, although I also realized what a terrible and often unwelcome burden being the eldest son was. I do not recall my father behaving as if Lathy would one day take over the jewellery shop, as was the custom with fathers and eldest sons, but it might have indeed been his hope and expectation. However, Lathy was still in boarding school (as was I) when the civil war began, and after that things went very badly for my father. So who knows?

Lathy didn't show any real interest in working at my father's shop, in any case. I think he was much more interested in striking out on his own. I do know, however, that my father expected Lathy to do his duty when it came to taking care of the family.

I seldom talked to my older brother. Whenever my mother thought I was being too familiar with him, or too free in my ways, talking back or arguing with him, she would scold me: "Respect your brother!"

Sometimes I would get beaten for taking things from Lathy. Because he was the eldest son, he got all the attention from everyone — our father, mother, uncles, aunts, grand-mothers, and grandfathers. My father bought him a bike on his tenth birthday, when I was just eight. I had always wanted to learn how to ride a bike, so I begged him to let me borrow it.

"First, you have to clean it and show it to me," he demanded.

I spent two hours cleaning his bike, including the rims, spokes, and tires. Then I used coconut oil to polish everything. He soon realized my potential and agreed to lend me the bike. The deal was that I had to clean it before taking it and upon returning it.

I was too young to properly respect my brother. All I wanted was to have fun and play. I was on much better terms with my younger brother, Kanna. Together, we could have fun that we weren't allowed to have with Lathy.

Construction on our family home had begun the year my mother and father were married. When I was born three years later, the house was finally finished and they moved in.

After my aunt had come to live with us, my father added the extension, and eventually our house consisted of two verandas with five rooms and two kitchens. We had an iron gate along with seven-foot-high concrete walls. We also had a German shepherd named Tony, who guarded our house day and night. The dog was two weeks old when my father brought him home, and I think giving him the name Tony had something to do with my father's love for Hollywood movies. My father hired a carpenter to have a shed built for the dog, and he arranged to have special milk delivered for Tony's bowl. Twice a week, Kanna and I went to the butcher shop to buy meat and then cooked it for him. He enjoyed his treat and played with us.

Years later, when the soldiers attacked our village, Tony hardly barked. He was quite old by that time. After the civil war had begun and times were hard and we were struggling to eat, my family could not afford to feed him. One day he ate a dead crow, became sick, and died. I had left Sri Lanka, at the time, and would learn about it in a letter from my mother. She said Kanna was devastated and mourned for months.

When my father was still successful, before the outbreak of the civil war, his driver, Hanny, would wash and polish our car six days a week. Hanny was very handy and would always drive us into the city when we needed a ride, although I usually biked. I tried to avoid Hanny because if I did something wrong — such as the time I made the mistake of eating with my father's employees, thus compromising his status — he would tell my father. The consequence of my misdeed was usually a beating with my father's belt.

In addition to Hanny, my father was wealthy enough to employ a servant. He was older than Hanny, shy and quiet. We called him Appa. He came from the Kandy tea-plantation area. He had a wife and child in Kandy, but we never met them. Twice a year, he left to visit his family. My father paid him well.

Both of the men had Sundays off. On those days, our father would take us to our favourite beach, Casuarina, for picnics. It was usually sweltering, so we would take a quick dip in the ocean to cool down. We did not swim like other children, though. My father considered swimming in the ocean an inappropriate activity for us. We loved playing along the shore and flying our kites. We ate lots of fish, crab, shrimp, and vegetables, but what I remember best from those Sunday picnics was the goat curry with rice. Cooked with fresh Sri Lankan spices, goat-meat curry has thick gravy with extra depth of colour. When my mother cooks it, I can smell it from miles away.

Our servant did most of the house chores, such as taking care of our plants, chopping firewood, and cleaning the yards. He did pretty much everything except cook and wash dishes. My mother did the cooking. She would often go to the market to buy fresh seafood and vegetables. At home, my father would eat only if my mother or aunt prepared and cooked the meals. My mother would stand next to him and serve him his food. Once he finished eating, she would give us children our meal, and then she would eat alone. Sometimes Kanna and I would eat with our servant. We treated him as part of our family.

In the village, everyone treated us differently because of my father's prominence. When we visited temples, the people would let our family go to the front, keeping their distance and standing behind us. When I travelled by bus or train, people — even older people — would offer me their seats.

I am ashamed when I remember this now, but I was too young at the time to understand what was going on or to question it.

Like my father, I had a head for numbers and was highly detail oriented. When I was ten years old, I managed to save about three hundred Sri Lankan rupees (about eleven U.S. dollars) in my bank account. It was a lot of money at the time, enough to feed a family like ours for a week.

Often, I would buy a variety of items in town at low prices and store them in a locked cabinet at home. With so many children underfoot, my mother was always in a hurry, so I would sell her "my groceries" for twice what I had paid. It was our little secret.

I was also something of a budding agriculturalist. I cleared a large patch of our backyard to plant chili, cassava, eggplant, long beans, and bitter melon. My younger brother, Kanna, was bigger and more muscular than I was. Because he loved doing outdoor work, I managed to convince him to be a partner in my business. He was delighted! What that meant was that he would do most of the clearing, digging, fertilizing, watering, and weeding; I would concentrate on management.

At first, it worked out well. The vegetables flourished and I had dreams of reaping a rich and profitable harvest. What I had not factored in to my business plan was my mother assuming the vegetable garden had been planted entirely for her benefit and convenience. It took a lot of time and energy to run a business at such a young age, and I felt it was my father's responsibility to provide for the family. When I saw my mother picking my vegetables for the family dinner, however, I realized I had no way of stopping her.

My other money-making schemes were even less successful. One summer day, I forced myself to wake up around 4:00 a.m., then went to cut down a banana tree. I had noticed that the tree in question had a rack of about two hundred bananas, but climbing it to cut down the rack seemed far more difficult than just cutting the whole tree down. It was hard work, but when the tree toppled over, I loaded the bananas onto the back of Lathy's bicycle and pedalled into town. I sold my bananas to a vendor at the fruit market and managed to bicycle back home before anyone else awoke. I pretended as if nothing had happened and went to school as usual.

That evening, though, my father came at me with his belt. I knew he was going to beat me, so I ran like mad straight at him. He was momentarily startled, and when he swung the belt, the buckle caught me on the calf of my right leg. I screamed with pain and hit the ground, grasping my leg. Blood began pooling on the floor.

When my father saw the gash on my leg, he went white as a sheet. My mother hurried into the room and pressed a cloth to my leg, and then the chauffeur drove the two of us to the hospital. Not my father. A doctor stitched my leg and I was sent home. My father was not there when we returned.

Later that night, my mother admitted that someone had informed my father that I had been seen selling bananas at the market. He had been furious, as it was shameful and a huge insult for the son of such a successful and respected man of the village to be selling fruit in a market. He was angry that we had lost respect.

For days after that, he avoided me. He never talked to me about what he had done; he never mentioned the incident.

I was angry, too, at first. Once I even exaggerated my limp, groaning, just to irritate him.

My brother Kanna and I played with our cousins often; we went to the beaches, played hide-and-seek in the bushes, flew kites, climbed trees, chased cows, and used slingshots to hit the squirrels. In the evenings, Kanna and I liked to ride our bikes to the shopping area in town and hang out with our cousin Suddy. Sometimes we went to the local cinemas and watched movies with Suddy and his friends and ate street foods: kothu roti, vadai, and sundal.

Kothu roti is chopped roti, a flatbread, combined with fried egg and seasoned mutton curry, which the vendors made in front of us in the street. The smell of the sizzling meat would make my mouth water. Vadai is a fried pastry, crispy on the outside but marvellously fluffy in the centre. We ate them plain or dipped them in coconut sambal and sambar. Coconut sambal is a mixture of grated coconut, dried red chillies, small onions, tamarind, and salt. Sambar is a thick gravy mix consisting of lentils and a variety of vegetables cooked with tamarind and other spices. Another delicious treat was sundal, made with chickpeas, grated mango, coconut, and chopped onion, which Suddy would buy for us from the vendors out in front of the cinemas.

Most of the movies we watched were from India, as the local cinema only played Tamil movies. If I wanted to see a European or American film, I had to wait for my father to take us into Jaffna. We usually did this on a Friday after visiting the temple. My father and I loved westerns and James Bond films. I especially liked *The Man with the Golden Gun*.

I didn't really understand what was going on, but it didn't seem to matter.

I looked forward to the Hindu festivals every year. Some lasted for days, and we would spend the whole night at the temple. Special guests from out of town would come and play barrel-shaped drums and nadaswaram, long classic wind instruments commonly played at Hindu weddings and at Hindu temples during festivals. We could hear the music from miles away.

The annual Nallur Festival runs for twenty-five days in August. Men and boys dress in bright white sarongs, while women wear colourful saris. The entire town of Jaffna and the Nallur Kandaswamy Temple are transformed to stage an intriguing event. At night, holy men pull a massive chariot around the town. The next day, devotees insert metal hooks through the flesh of their backs in honour of the gods and carry a kavadi (a semicircular wooden box decorated with colourful ornaments and peacock feathers) on their shoulders. They dance on the streets while drums and nadaswaram are played. In some instances, the hooks are attached to a pole and the pole attached to the front of a tractor. The tractor drives the worshippers through town before heading to the temple. A person stands at one end of the pole and rocks it up and down like puppeteer with a gigantic puppet or a fisherman with a wiggling fish. According to custom, the devotee puts his palms together and chants *arohara* over and over. This is a short form of *ara haro hara*, which means "Oh God Almighty, please remove our sufferings and grant us salvation."

The devotees who carry the kavadi are people who have been cured of an illness and have promised to perform a ritual of self-mortification as tribute. According to my mother, a devotee never feels any pain. My older brother, Lathy, carried a kavadi once after he was cured of chicken pox. He was about eight years old at the time, and my mother had promised God that if he were cured, he would carry the kavadi. This kind of practice was very common when I was growing up. He had to dance to the music with the kavadi on his shoulder. Although it may have been painful, we were happy that he had kept my mother's promise to God.

Every year, my brothers and I would save money for eleven months, then spend it all during the festival. We would buy toys, statues, pictures of God and movie stars, sweets, and sodas. There were no toy stores in our town, so Kanna and I would make our own toys. We would nail a tin lid to a stick to roll along the street or place soda-bottle caps on the train tracks and wait for the train to pass. Once a cap was flattened, I would make two holes in the middle, insert a long string and tie a knot, and then hold the ends of the string to make it spin, like a chainsaw.

Kanna was a good sport. He would sit inside an old tire and I would roll him down the street. It was great fun.

But it wouldn't be long before everything changed.

CHAPTER 8

This country belongs to the Sinhalese, and it is the Sinhalese
who built up its civilisation, culture and settlements.
— Galagoda Aththe Gnanasara Thero,
Buddhist monk, to a BBC reporter, May 30, 2015

On May 18, 2009, the brutal twenty-six-year ethnic
conflict known as the Sri Lankan civil war officially
ended. Depending on who is consulted, the war
between the majority Sinhalese and the minority Tamils killed
more than one hundred thousand civilians and a total of more
than fifty thousand government soldiers and armed rebels.
The United Nations concluded that as many as forty thousand
Tamil civilians were killed by government forces in the bloody

final stage of the conflict alone. Acts of genocide, it reported, were perpetrated on both sides, but it singled out Tamil civilians as the most abused victims.

As with most wars, there was nothing civil about it. In a civil war, winners are often difficult to distinguish from losers; no side truly wins. Even when it is over, it isn't really over. Not for everyone, anyway. Allegations of assault, rape, and torture against the Sri Lankan security forces continued to circulate years after the war ended. Evidence "strongly suggested the abuse was widespread and systematic," according to a Human Rights Watch report in 2013.

When I was growing up, the majority Sinhalese strongly resented the presence of Tamils, whom they dismissed as undesirable. They saw the Tamils as newcomers who took much and contributed nothing to the country. Today, it is not nearly as bad as it was back then, but the peace is still fragile. The war is over and the situation in the North has improved, but the mental trauma has not disappeared. The Sinhalese remain the majority population in Sri Lanka, and — as has been said many times — history is written by the winners.

The Tamils have always maintained strong cultural and religious beliefs. A Hindu ethnic group from southern India, Tamils at the time of the civil war made up 20 percent of Sri Lanka's population; the Sinhalese, a Buddhist ethnic group, accounted for 75 percent of the total population. The remaining 5 percent consisted mostly of Muslims and Christians.

The truth is, Tamils have been in Sri Lanka for centuries. But so what? What difference does it make how long a people has been here or there? Or that one is a Hindu and another is a Buddhist? Isn't it more important *who* we are?

I was born and raised among Tamils. Tamils were all I knew, and I was — still am — extremely proud of my Tamil heritage. Before the civil war, being a Tamil was not even an issue. I never thought about it. Politics was never discussed at home. My father, as a prosperous, well-respected business-man, focused less on the status of Tamil ethnic identity and the issue of Tamil independence and more on the practical demands of sustaining profits and maintaining his status. I expect that some of his higher-official friends, with whom he conducted business, were Sinhalese, and it made no sense to make enemies.

To be honest, as a boy, I was less aware of being Tamil than I was of being treated differently because of my family's wealth and status. It was odd to me, for instance, that my father dis-couraged us from swimming at the beach like other children. He associated swimming with fishermen and other labourers. Unfortunately, at that time, the caste system was still a fact of life in Sri Lanka, and when one grows up with a certain arrangement, it is easy to think that this is the way it is every-where — the way life is supposed to be.

And because of the way I grew up, I was naive about many things. For instance, it would have been extremely unusual for my mother to engage with my father on issues of politics. A wife would never presume to debate her hus-band or even offer an opinion unless asked to do so. I am quite sure my father never asked. I have no idea what she thought about the majority Sinhalese. I doubt she knew any Sinhalese people. As a proper Hindu wife, she observed strict obedience to my father, as she fulfilled her role of complete devotion to him and her family. Still, she was intelligent, and I wonder what she thought about the situation in Sri

Lanka. She was obsessively protective of her children and would shelter us from any threat.

I grew up in a cocoon, essentially immunized from any direct experience with the ethnic rivalries that would inevitably tear the country apart. It wasn't until I was twelve years old, when I enrolled at boarding school in Jaffna, that I first began hearing stories of Sinhalese attacks on Tamils. In fact, the closer the country moved to war, the more Tamil families who lived in places like Colombo, the capital of Sri Lanka, were moving to Jaffna to enroll their children in Tamil schools. The city boys in my class would tell stories of Tamils being attacked and beaten by Sinhalese mobs or of family members being arrested at night and taken away by soldiers.

Before boarding school, however, my friends and I never really talked about it. My period of sheltered isolation lasted until 1981, when Sinhalese thugs went on a rampage and burned the famous Jaffna Library to the ground. It was my first experience with cultural genocide.

Tamils will insist that they have deep roots in Sri Lanka.

Anti-Tamil Sinhalese tend to dispute the claim that Tamils have a respected history in the country, insisting that Tamils are recent "outsiders" who flooded into Sri Lanka from India to work as cheap labourers on British tea plantations. Not surprisingly, the truth is somewhere in between and far more complex.

Not only do Sri Lankan Tamils have a rich cultural legacy, they have a well-earned reputation for prizing education and, most especially, literacy.

When the Portuguese conquered what was then known as the Kingdom of Jaffna (essentially northern Sri Lanka) in the early fifteenth century, they brought with them the rudiments of Western-style education. The number of schools was increased, and the schools were expanded when the Dutch ousted the Portuguese and the Jesuits.

The missionary schools created and run by the Jesuits later became the template for schools teaching large numbers of Tamil students. Interestingly, it was the widespread success, growth, and popularity of the missionary schools and their attempts to promote Christianity that, by the middle of the nineteenth century, provoked a nationalist backlash among Tamils, who wanted to establish Tamil-based schools and colleges. Tamils were both creating a sense of ethnic identity and solidarity and raising educational standards across the board.

When the British wrested colonial control of Ceylon from the Dutch in 1796, effective administration required the services of thousands of literate native Sri Lankans to work as civil servants and administrators. This angered the majority Sinhalese, however, as the better-educated and highly literate Tamils were appointed to prestigious and well-paying government positions in far higher numbers. It is possible, too, that the British favoured the minority Tamils as a strategic counterpoint to any revolt by the majority Sinhalese.

In any case, the tables turned in 1948 when control of Ceylon was relinquished by the British. The country was renamed Sri Lanka, and the majority Sinhalese — their anger still festering over the favouritism they believed the British had shown to the minority Tamils — embarked on their path to avenge what they perceived as years of injustice.

A few years earlier, a motion had been presented to the ruling congress to establish Sinhala as the official language, replacing English. It did not pass, but the stage had been set for conflict.

Tensions between the Tamils and Sinhalese escalated dramatically after 1948. Shortly after independence, more than seven hundred thousand ethnic Indian Tamils living in Ceylon were made stateless when parliament passed the Ceylon Citizenship Act, which made citizenship in Sri Lanka incredibly difficult for Indian Tamils to obtain. It is estimated that as many as three hundred thousand Tamils were forced to return to India as a result.

In 1956, Sinhala did become the official language of Sri Lanka, an act that outraged Tamils, most of whom did not speak Sinhala and who, therefore, either were forced to resign or found themselves suddenly ineligible for employment in any civil-service capacity. The Sinhala Only Act drove the wedge between the two ethnic groups even deeper. Tamils decried what they declared was blatant discrimination by the majority government. In response to the act, Tamil political leaders called for nonviolent resistance. When riots erupted in June 1956, hundreds of Tamils were killed, and the Sinhalese government hastily negotiated a compromise settlement with the Tamils that would have made Tamil the official administrative language in Tamil-majority areas of Sri Lanka. However, pressure from Sinhalese nationalists overturned the agreement.

Tensions flared in communities around the country, and at least a thousand Tamils were killed in riots that broke out, particularly in the east and north. The prime minister fanned the flames of anger and resentment among the Sinhalese by blaming the Tamils for the murder of a local mayor. Tamils were also rumoured to have been responsible for a horrible attack that left a teacher mutilated. Sinhalese gangs bent on revenge responded by attacking Tamils whenever and wherever they could be found. Even Sinhalese who sheltered Tamils were hunted down and threatened, beaten, or killed. Properties owned by Tamils were looted and burned down by Sinhalese mobs. These atrocities rendered around twelve thousand Tamils in Colombo homeless.

While mobs attacked Tamil citizens, the government refused to act. Five days after the riots began, the government declared a state of emergency.

In 1958, the Tamil Language Act was passed, but it would prove to be too little too late. The army was withdrawn, except in Jaffna. In effect, Tamils were under a state of permanent siege.

But I was aware of virtually none of this when I was growing up. And knowing why the civil war broke out would not have made a difference. When a person is pointing a gun at you, does it really matter why?

CHAPTER 9

You don't have to be great to start,
but you have to start to be great.
— Joe Sabah

When I was twelve years old, my parents sent me to St. John's College, a boarding school in Jaffna. The school followed British curriculum, standards, and policies. We lived by the clock, and it felt like I was in a military school. A wrinkled bed or a late arrival at class or meals would be met with consequences: after-school detention, loss of home-visit privileges, a slap in the face, or a beating with guava sticks. If we accumulated too many infractions, we had to face the principal, and it wasn't pretty. He had a vast collection of canes and loved to use every one. Most of us followed the rules.

On my first day, my father and mother drove me to the school and parked our shiny white Peugeot 404 in front of an older building. A senior boy standing by the entrance greeted us. He was the prefect and in charge of the dormitory. He had a private room beside the entrance.

My new surroundings were very different from home. Instead of rooms, the dormitory had two sections, front and back. It looked more like a warehouse than sleeping quarters, with about forty beds lined up one next to another. I was assigned to the Evarts Hostel.

I noticed a couple of other boys sitting on their beds, crying. They looked much younger than me, and it turned out they were only in grade four. I was attending grade six. But I felt like crying, too.

My mother prepared my bed as my father put my suitcase away in a communal area at the back. "Kavanamaka padik-kavum," she whispered to me, with tears in her eyes. *Study carefully*. I felt tears in my eyes, too. A few minutes later, my parents said goodbye and left.

I was overcome with loneliness. It was the first time in my life I had been on my own. I sat down on the bed, nervously wondering how I was going to survive in such strange and hostile surroundings.

My eldest brother, Lathy, was a student at the same school. But as a new boy, I was required to arrive early for orientation; Lathy wouldn't arrive for another few days. Lucky for me, another boy came up to me after a while and asked me my name. I quickly wiped my face, brushing away my tears. I was embarrassed to be acting like a grade-four boy. He introduced himself as Shiran, and we started talking.

He was from Colombo, he said.

"Do you know anyone here in Jaffna?" I asked.

"Not really," he said.

He pulled a bag of Smarties from his pocket and offered me some. Shiran was my first friend at boarding school.

Later that first day, a bell rang and the prefect entered the dormitory and commanded us to dinner. Actually, it wasn't so much the bell that rallied us as it was a fellow from the dining-hall staff furiously banging a piece of steel bar from a railway track with a long pipe.

We all filed into the dining room, a featureless but spacious hall lined with tables and benches. I was told that the first two tables were reserved for vegetarians. Hindus are not allowed to eat meat, especially beef — cows are sacred animals in Hinduism — so I sat at the first table. We were instructed that every boy must eat everything on his plate before anyone was allowed to leave. Every table was assigned a monitor to ensure that we were following the rules. Otherwise, the prefect warned us bluntly, we would be disciplined.

At the end of each day, the warden of our dormitory, Mr. Ponniah, entered the dormitory and summarized the day. During these summaries boys would be notified of any demerits they had earned for mischievous or unacceptable behaviour. Some infractions were minor and warranted nothing more severe than a warning and a few demerits or a short time in detention. Punishments often were served by writing out things like "I will keep my bed clean all the time" one thousand times on lined papers. Other misdemeanours were more serious and could result in a boy being caned and/or expelled from school. Lathy was expelled once because he had left school without permission to come home. My father had been furious with him and had to use his influence to plead with the principal to allow him to return.

I had no wish to offend my father, so I did my best to toe the line when it came to the rules. I wasn't like Lathy in that respect. He had a much deeper rebellious streak. Perhaps this is common in eldest sons.

Life in a boarding school is ruled by routine — mind-numbing routine. We were awakened at 5:30 in the morning and had mandatory prayers at 6:15. Study hall commenced fifteen minutes later, at 6:30 on the dot. We were called to breakfast at 7:45. Morning classes began at 8:30 and lasted until the 12:45 lunch break. Then more classes until 15:45, with sports afterward at 16:00. More studies at 18:15, then prayers at 19:45. After dinner, we went to bed and lights out by 21:00. As we moved to the upper years, we ended up studying much longer and instead went to bed at 23:00.

The thing about boarding school is this: one learns the ropes quickly. It was disorienting at first, but I learned I had to do everything by myself: waking up on time, making my bed, bathing, dressing for school, doing my homework, washing and folding my clothes, and so on.

I was uniquely inept at sports and joined the Scout Club instead. Occasionally, I played carom, a game similar to billiards but played on a much smaller table and using fingers instead of cues. Once I even won the runner-up prize for singles. I also participated in stage dramas, but I could never remember my lines when it counted, so eventually I was relegated to appearing in crowd scenes, where it did not matter if I flubbed or forgot a line.

The year was punctuated by major school events. The Battle of the North was the annual cricket match between Jaffna Central College and St. John's College, two leading schools in Jaffna. The match was played over three days and the school ground was filled with current and former students, parents, and other spectators from all over town. The cricket fans would carry their school flags, beat drums, and dance around the city on match days to show their support.

The annual boarders' day event was also a big deal, and we would start preparing for it a couple of months in advance. Actually a week-long celebration, it was filled with singing, dramas, various sports, memory games, eating competitions between hostels, and other events. Boarders' day itself was on the Saturday, and the students would all have dinner on the school grounds with the principal, wardens, and their families. During that time, prizes were given to the winners of the week's events, and then we would sing, dance, and tell jokes. I recall it as one of my happiest times at boarding school.

The food at the school was mostly unremarkable and often horrible, so we spent a lot of time dawdling at the gate, begging non-boarders to buy us food from Cheryl's Café, the shop across from the school. Boarders were never allowed to leave school premises unless we had explicit permission. Every boarder was given two absits and two exeats per term. Absits allowed a student to be absent from the college for up to two hours. We used them for shopping trips and for buying snacks in town, or sometimes to go to one of the movie theatres. The masters and prefects were always on the lookout, watching like crows, for boys returning late from an absit. Exeats were for weekend home visits.

I thought of home a lot. Although I made many wonderful friends at school, the loneliness that seemed to be at my core never completely went away. I missed my mother's delicious cooking. I was worried about my mother, of course, and about my younger brother and sisters. Often, I would lie awake at night wondering how they were getting along. Was my father treating my mother well?

My parents visited me at school, usually once a month on a Sunday. My father would drive up with my mother. I always looked forward to those visits because my mother brought home-cooked meals. Very often I would sit down right then and eat what she had brought. Other times I would share it with my friends, all of us huddled over parcels of food, scooping with our bare hands, desperate for a taste of home.

On those Sunday afternoons, my father was usually very formal. He would ask me about my school marks and occasionally, when I showed him my interim report card, he would check over it and say, "This is very good." And that was about it. He and my mother would stay for a couple of hours. Once a week, boarders were required to write letters home. I never received any return letters from my parents.

I was restless; I did not really feel at home at boarding school the way some boys seemed to. I wanted to go home and spend time with my mother and have a break from school, but I was afraid of my father and unsure of how he would react. Around this time I found out that he was drinking more than before, and there was vague talk about the business not doing well. More worrisome, my father was fighting with my mother and with my aunt.

At school, I was a natural in mathematics and science but hated humanities and anything to do with art. On my O-level exams, I got five distinctions, in mathematics, science, health, commerce, and Hinduism, and three credits, in

English, Tamil, and social studies. I became exhausted from the pressure of endless studying. The atmosphere was competitive and achievement was compulsory. All students at the hostel were required to have monthly performance reports signed by the principal. Even a slight drop in achievement from one month to the next resulted in a painful caning of the backside. Doing well was not enough; a boy who did well was required to continue to do well — or to do even better.

There were many times when I was so frustrated and upset that I threatened to quit. I dreamed of running away. It didn't matter where. On the other hand, I was very proud of my accomplishments and wanted to work as hard as I could to be the best. This meant, however, many hours locked away by myself to study.

Looking back, I think in those years I was suffering from depression. I see now that I began to separate myself from my friends. I squirrelled myself away in my books; I avoided sports as much as I could. I lost interest in just about everything other than academics.

CHAPTER 10

Books are the carriers of civilization. Without books,
history is silent, literature dumb, science crippled,
thought and speculation at a standstill.
— Barbara W. Tuchman

I was only six years old in 1972 when the various Tamil
political parties in northern and eastern Sri Lanka voted
to combine into what became known as the Tamil United
Liberation Front (TULF). A few years later, the front voted to
demand from the ruling congress a separate Tamil state, Tamil
Eelam. Also in 1972, a Tamil group was formed that would
eventually be transformed into the Liberation Tigers of Tamil
Eelam (LTTE) guerrilla group.

Of course, I was not aware of these things at the time. Events in Colombo might as well have been a million miles away. What I do remember, however, was an increasing presence of government soldiers in the area around our village. I also began to hear about the freedom fighters. That was not what the government called them. To the government they were rebels and needed to be put down, like rabid dogs. The soldiers I remember were always standoffish, aloof, and suspicious of Tamils. Mostly I tried to stay as far away from the soldiers as I could. I tried to make myself invisible to them.

I have no recollection of ever meeting a rebel when I was young, but I imagined these freedom fighters must be good and honourable men. After all, who could be against freedom for Tamils? To a boy of my age, the whole thing sounded very exciting.

Another wave of riots erupted in 1977 after the general elections, in which the TULF won a majority of the minority Tamil vote. The TULF was advocating openly for a separate Tamil state, and Prime Minister Junius Jayewardene blamed the TULF for a number of attacks on soldiers and security forces by so-called separatist militants.

The government's response was swift and deliberate: supporters of separatist political parties were arrested, and thousands — a majority of whom were Indian Tamil plantation workers — were forced from their homes, many of which were then looted and destroyed. It is estimated that as many as seventy-five thousand Tamils were made homeless in the aftermath of the riots.

But on May 31, 1981, when I was fifteen years old, the civil war became devastatingly real for me.

74

The Jaffna Public Library had been built in 1933 to retain Tamil literature and culture. At the time, it was one of the largest libraries in Asia, housing ninety-seven thousand books and precious ancient manuscripts containing irreplaceable artifacts of Tamil cultural and historical heritage.

For me — for every Tamil — the Jaffna Library was a cultural landmark of immense importance. Originally just two storeys, it had been enlarged over the years until it became one of the finest and most respected libraries in all of Asia. Researchers from around the world made use of its rich archival holdings, many of its manuscripts dating back thousands of years.

The first time I saw it, as a child, I thought it was immense, even triumphant. Surrounded by beautiful and exotic gardens, it rose up to the sky like an enormous white palace. At night, in the moonlight, it shone like a beacon in the darkness. A statue of Saraswathi, a Hindu goddess of education, stood at the front of the library, welcoming visitors. Seeing Saraswathi always made me smile; as a Tamil, I felt so proud.

The library was less than twenty minutes walking distance from St. John's College. The bell in our residence rang, as usual, at 5:45 a.m. I groaned, rubbed my eyes, and rolled over, holding my pillow over my head, wondering how long I could sleep before our warden bounded in with his usual "Wake up, boys!"

But that day, when our warden rushed in, he was breathing hard and his face was twisted in panic. Immediately, we knew something was wrong.

"Boys! Listen to me!"

We became scared; the warden looked terrified.

"Our Jaffna Library is on fire!"

We responded with an eerie silence. *What? What do you mean? How can it be on fire?* It didn't make sense.

"Please!" He clapped his hands, spurring us into action. "We need all of you to help put out the fire!"

Many of us did not even bother throwing on our clothes. We jumped up and ran out in our nightclothes and bare feet as fast as we could to the library down the street.

When I arrived at the scene, the sky was a sickly yellow, thick with smoke. The smell was acrid and intense.

It is true, I thought to myself. In the distance, dark smoke clotted like small clouds. The force of the heat was so intense, it was as if it was threatening us not to get any closer. People scurried like ants on an anthill in all directions. Bucket brigades were forming, as chains of people passed buckets of sloshing water and attempted to put out the fire. Others fought to get inside the building to save books. It was hopeless. Most of the building was already in flames. There was absolutely nothing we could do.

My friends and I looked at each other, our hands on our heads, swearing "Aiyoo Kadavulai!" *Oh God!* The fire seemed like a huge, angry beast, ravenous and insatiable, consuming itself. The flames licked up the walls, crackled, and spat like exploding stars; the smoke was searing and choking. Policemen kept anyone from approaching the fire. Rumours spread quickly that they were actually there to prevent people from trying to put out the fire. By the time the fire had burned itself out, virtually nothing of the Jaffna Library remained. It had burned literally to the ground. Everything was lost.

I felt like part of me had been taken away, a part of us, the Tamil people. It was as if my entire biography — my history and the history of all Tamils — had been destroyed, wiped from the face of the Earth as if we did not exist.

Saraswathi stood as protector among a pile of ruins.

The national newspapers were not permitted to print anything about the burning of the Jaffna Library. As far as the majority Sinhalese were concerned, nothing had happened.

We later learned that the burning of the library had been an act of retaliation by the government for the deaths of two Sinhalese policemen killed at a TULF rally the day before. Supposedly, police and security forces, with the eager assistance of mobs of outraged Sinhalese, had set the fire. The office of a local newspaper had also been destroyed, as had the offices of the TULF and the home of Jaffna's Tamil minister of parliament.

As it did for many Tamils, especially Tamils my age, the burning of the Jaffna Library struck me deep in my core. It seemed so senseless — so cruel and vindictive and unnecessary.

I kept thinking to myself, *Why?*

CHAPTER 11

On July 23, 1983, fifteen Sri Lankan soldiers were killed in a nighttime ambush by members of the LTTE near Jaffna. A bomb exploded near a Jeep, and when the convoy came to a halt, Tamil Tigers opened fire on the soldiers with automatic rifles and grenades.

The majority Sinhalese naturally considered the attack a brutal and unprovoked act of terrorism. To the Tamil Tigers, it was a justified response to numerous government-sanctioned pogroms against an oppressed minority. More specifically, the Tigers claimed that their attack was retaliation for the alleged abduction and rape of Tamil schoolgirls.

Civil war had begun.

In what became known as Black July, a violent week of anti-Tamil riots erupted around the country. They would render 150,000 people homeless and as many as 2,500 dead. Thousands of shops and homes were destroyed, and hundreds of millions of dollars of damage was done to the economy. Many Tamils fled to the North, the Tamil-majority region.

I was still asking myself why. Only now, it didn't matter. It was too late for whys.

It was difficult at the time to find out what was going on. Tamil printing companies and newspapers had been either burned or shut down. The upper-year students at St. John's College had built pocket FM radios from kits, so my classmates and I bought radios from them to listen to the news and dramas without fear of being caught by the warden and prefects.

Our teachers, of course, were in a panic. Should they continue classes? Should they shut down the school and send the boys home? It was very confusing for the students because none of the teachers wanted to talk about it.

Later, I learned that government officials had provided the voter lists to the mobs, which is how they were able to identify Tamil-owned properties to destroy and Tamil people to kill during the riots.

When we heard the news about Black July on the radio, my classmates and I were devastated and afraid. The parents of my friend Nishan were living in the Anderson Flats neighbourhood of Colombo, which had been attacked by a mob of thugs bent on revenge. They were able to escape safely because their block was occupied mainly by Sinhalese actors and government officials.

Rumours spread like wildfire, and because the country's news media were controlled by the majority Sinhalese, the Tamils were blamed for the rioting and the violence. The Sinhalese were portrayed as merely protecting themselves, and nothing was reported of police and security forces encouraging mobs to attack Tamil civilians.

It took many months before things started to get back to normal. But it wasn't like before. It couldn't be. You would see people here and there in the city, but more and more people stayed home whenever they could and avoided places like markets or train stations.

Large numbers of soldiers moved into Jaffna.

At my school, enrolment jumped, with Tamil students from Colombo hoping to escape the worst of the violence. Curfews had been imposed in Jaffna and often classes were cancelled. Most of the students from the boarding school stayed at the hostel. It was safer than living outside of school.

Ever since the riots, the government had banned local live broadcasts of all television and radio programs, so we only heard bits and pieces from India BBC News and my Colombo friends. We were miserable because we were worried about home and our parents and siblings. By the time school got back to normal, we were overloaded with work. When we didn't have classes, we would head to the study room.

The Sinhalese hatred of Tamils only worsened after the Tamil Tigers declared war on the Sri Lankan government on July 23, 1983, beginning a bloody and senseless conflict that lasted almost three decades. The war was filled with intense suicide bombing campaigns by Tamil Tigers. The Sri Lankan Army retaliated by attacking Tamil Tigers, as well as by displacing or killing many innocent Tamil civilians. War crimes were suspected on both sides before the Tamil Tigers were finally defeated in 2009. Every Sri Lankan, both Tamils and Sinhalese, lived in fear for a very long time. Many do still.

Hatred is a hard enemy to defeat.

CHAPTER 12

Once a month during the school term, the students were allowed to return home for a weekend visit.

One Friday in March of 1984, I was anxious to go home and see my family. I was looking forward to having home-cooked meals and hanging out with my cousins. After class, I went to see my warden for permission to leave. He had a private room, which was part of the dormitory. I knocked at the door.

"Who is it?" he asked.

"This is Logathasan, sir! I would like to go home for the weekend."

I needed him to sign my exeats card.

I heard him stomp across the floor. The door swung open. "You must come back by Sunday night!" he said by way of greeting.

I nodded. "Yes, sir."

I handed him my exeats card. He took a pen from his front pocket and wrote the date and time and then initialled my card. He handed it back without a word.

"Thank you, sir," I said.

He nodded noncommittally and shut the door. I took the card and ran back to the main part of the dormitory. I changed out of my uniform, packed my bag, and then headed to the Jaffna railway station, less than a mile from St. John's College.

After a twenty-minute walk, I arrived at the station and went up to the counter to buy a ticket to Chavakachcheri. I waited impatiently at the platform. After what seemed an eternity, but was at most a few minutes, the train pulled into the station and I hopped aboard. The car was empty except for a group of soldiers at the front. It was too late for me to move to another car; I didn't want to attract suspicion, so I walked in the opposite direction and sat down next to a window and thought only of how much I was looking forward to being home.

At that time, tensions between Tamils and Sinhalese were ratcheting up. Only a few days earlier, the military had killed nine Tamil civilians in what became known as the Chunnakam market massacre. Two months earlier, twenty Tamil civilians had been killed in another military attack. The military presence was very high in Jaffna. Trains and buses were a favourite target for rebels, according to the government, and it was common for soldiers or security forces to be posted inside trains, searching for Tamil rebels and sympathizers.

Not long after the train left the station, the group of soldiers walked down the aisle in my direction. I pretended to
look intently out the window. When they reached my seat,
they stopped. One soldier looked at me and said something.
He was not smiling, but his voice did not sound angry either.
The other soldiers around him began to laugh, however, and I
half-smiled, pretending to play along. *He must be teasing me,* I
thought to myself, as I did not speak Sinhala.

He said something else and sat down next to me. As he
did, his hand brushed the top of my shorts. He was very dark
and had spooky, dead eyes. When he opened his mouth, I saw
his yellow teeth. He must have been about thirty.

Instinctively I crossed my legs and turned my head away
to stare fixedly out the window at the landscape whizzing by.
Empty pastures as far as the eye could see, rocks, withered trees
under a hot sky.

The gesture angered him. He turned aggressive. I felt the soldier's powerful hand wedge my legs open. I stiffened, tried to wrig-
gle away. I was terrified of making him angrier. I would not look at
him. He pushed his hand inside my shorts. I felt his hand on me.
Squeezing tenderly, stroking, attempting to induce an erection.

I was biting the inside of my mouth so hard I could taste
blood. I was praying it would stay limp; maybe the soldier
would tire of me and lose interest. The harder I tried to banish
from my mind the reality of what was happening, the harder
it was to ignore it.

At one point I tried to push away his hand, but he rebuked
me sharply and squeezed hard. He rubbed his hand over me,
up and down.

I whimpered. I did not know what to do. If I struggled, I
was sure the other soldiers would join to help him. I released

my hand from his arm, pulling my arms close to my chest, withdrawing, thinking, *Better this than being beaten up or killed.*

When I ejaculated, the other soldiers jeered and hooted. The soldier looked at me, disgusted. He reached into his bag and withdrew a soiled sarong and tossed it into my lap.

I stared at the dirty sarong in my lap.

"A present!" he barked in a mocking tone. Then he uttered something in Sinhala which I didn't understand. The other soldiers burst out laughing. He stood up and walked away. The other soldiers fell in line and trooped obediently behind like trained dogs.

I stared out the window of the train at a landscape I had known since I was a child, as familiar as the back of my hand. But now it appeared alien, foreign, monstrous.

Then I saw the sign: CHAVAKACHCHERI.

I was near home.

I walked along the train tracks for a while, not thinking. The sun was about to disappear when I arrived home and saw my mother standing at the entrance to our house.

She was beaming. "Rajan! Ennada, indaiku vittai vantuvidai!" *Rajan, you are home today.*

I walked into my home feeling like a convict being led to the gallows.

"I have made your favourite meal!" my mother said.

I shook my head. "I am not hungry."

She asked me what was wrong.

I smiled. "Nothing, Amma. Nothing is wrong. Everything is fine."

CHAPTER 13

After I was molested on the train, I found my emotions swinging from one extreme to another. I was confused and I hated everything around me. My whole life had been turned upside down and I didn't know what to do or whom to tell. I doubted my ability to defend myself. What would I do if soldiers came near me again? I was desperately lonely and I isolated myself from everyone.

Fighting between the Tamil rebels and the army continued to escalate, and due to the curfews that had been imposed in Tamil zones by the government, boarding schools were often shut down without notice. Even when school was open, negotiating checkpoints along the roads to and from school became increasingly difficult.

I started skipping school and staying with my aunt. I didn't tell my parents. Instead of attending classes, I hung out with my childhood friends from Chavakachcheri Hindu College in my village. My cousins were disappeared. Some of them joined the rebels and others were captured and/or killed by soldiers. After a few weeks, I stopped going to school altogether. What was the point?

It turned out not to matter, in any case. My father had stopped making payments to my boarding school. Had I gone back to school, the principal probably would have asked me to leave anyway.

After Black July in 1983, my father's business had begun to fall apart. The civil war had made commerce extremely difficult. The army and civilians often clashed in street riots, and fewer and fewer customers could be found shopping the market areas. Curfews were frequent, which dampened trade further. Often, my father was forced to keep the shop closed for days or weeks at a time because of violence on the streets.

At one point he was forced to pawn jewellery from the store to keep the business afloat. Before long, he had virtually no inventory left. Everything was owned by the pawn shops. He must have borrowed quite a bit of money as well, as we found out that he had begun selling off large parcels of land to settle his debts. But because of the war, land values had plummeted, and what he received was a fraction of the value before the war.

But he never talked about his business at home, so as far as I knew, everything was fine. I am not sure if he discussed any details with my mother, but it seems unlikely. I did notice that he was more irritable than usual. He and my mother would have words, and I would hear arguments between him and my aunt, too. I think my father had been very generous with my aunt — it must have been one of the reasons she agreed to live with him as a mistress — so when money became tight, it created terrible friction. My mother never complained, of course, and made do as best she could.

My father was drinking a lot. At first it might have been casual, his effort to "keep up appearances" with his clients and business acquaintances. But the more he lost, the more he drank — and the more my mother struggled to maintain a calm and devoted demeanour. It became common for us to see him drinking at breakfast. His arguments with my mother became increasingly angrier; a few times he even hit her. He lost all interest in the family and seemed lost in bitter and angry self-pity.

One time he did not come home from work for days. I searched for him everywhere. Finally I found him, drunk, sleeping on the kitchen floor of my auntie's (my grandmother's sister) house in Jaffna. When I attempted to rouse him, he resisted violently and we fell into an argument. He swung out with his arm and caught me, hard, on the chin. It staggered me, nearly knocking me over. I was angry and hurt and nearly blind with tears. Looking at my father — this "important man" — drunk and dirty, slumped on the floor in a stupor, I had never felt so humiliated in my life. Wanting to hurt him as much as he had hurt me, I reached for a box of pesticide sitting on a shelf.

I swallowed the pesticide in front of my father.

Immediately, I felt the hot burn in my throat. I began choking and gasping for breath. It felt like my throat was being scraped by a rasp. I felt my stomach turn inside out, convulsing. Light-headed, I sank to the floor, clutching at my throat and chest.

Despite the pain, I found some satisfaction in the fact that he saw me crumple to the ground. *There!* I thought miserably. *This is what you have done to me. I hope you are happy now!*

I tried to speak. After a few moments, I realized I could not move. My arms and legs were frozen. I could hear Auntie's daughters screaming for help. I have a vague memory of my father and a neighbour lifting me from the ground, like a sack of potatoes, but I do not remember anything after that. When I woke up at the hospital, my throat was raw and painful and it hurt horribly to even swallow. I began to cry.

My mother was standing next to me, holding my hand and weeping. I remember noticing that she hadn't combed her hair. She looked drawn and very sad. When I saw my father, I turned my head away and ignored him. I was still furious with him. I didn't know how long I had been asleep at the hospital, but I was released the next day. They asked me to sign a few forms. I don't remember why or what they were for, but I signed. I didn't care.

Anger quickly turned to shame. I realized that because of my impulsiveness I could have died. Did I really think suicide was a solution? I was ashamed that I was not able — that I had not tried — to do more for my mother. I felt guilty about what she had been forced to endure. I should have been more supportive of my mother and helped my brothers and sisters. It was selfish of me to think only of myself, as my father seemed to be doing. *No,* I decided, stiffening my resolve. *I will not surrender.* I would never be so foolish again.

Nothing changed, however. In fact, the situation at home continued to deteriorate. Our village now resembled a ghost town. People were afraid to be outside or to socialize. The threat of the soldiers returning was constant, and so were the endless rumours: the schools were occupied by soldiers, who had converted them to military camps. The hospitals were being used by military personnel. Tamil boys and men were captured on the spot and transported to military camps for torture. I heard that some of torture included iron rods coated in chili powder being inserted into the prisoners' rectums and victims being hung upside down as their captors drilled holes into their bodies.

Curfews were established in Chavakachcheri, and the roadblocks and checkpoints along the highways meant that transport slowed to a crawl. Shelves at the shops and market stalls were bare; day by day it became harder to find food. Children would wander the village or town — even the fields — searching for anything that could be eaten or traded for food.

We lived just one day at a time. And each day was harder than the day before. In order to support his drinking, my father began selling off our furniture, the sewing machine, fridge, stove, light fixtures — basically, whatever he could find. Then he pawned all of my mother's jewellery, and then even her saris.

Our family had suddenly toppled from one of the most respected in town to absolute outcasts, even pariahs. The people who used to respect us turned their backs on us. The vendors and small-store owners who used to depend on our patronage shut their doors on us. We couldn't borrow anything anymore. Ironically, cash and gold had become worthless. Who could afford either? Bartering for food and drink became the main economy during the war.

In January 1984, a few months after I was chased through the rice paddies by the military helicopter and a couple of months before I was molested on the train, Lathy disappeared.

We had not been that close to begin with, and he was often away from home for long periods of time — staying with aunts, for instance, so he could be closer to school — but one day I realized it had been quite some time since I had seen him. In Tamil culture, it is normal for the eldest son to take over if the father is absent or incapacitated. Lathy, however, was nowhere to be found.

"Where is Lathy?" I asked my mother one afternoon.

"Away," she said.

That was curious. "Where?"

"France," she said. I waited for her to elaborate, but she said no more.

France, I thought. *What is he doing in France when he is supposed to be here, helping take care of us?*

I am the second son of the family. By default, therefore, I was now responsible for taking care of my mother, brother, and sisters. Not to mention a bitter and destitute alcoholic father who was drinking himself to death. I was very angry. Who did Lathy think he was? It was so unfair. What gave him the right to run off to France while I was stuck here? I had no idea how I could take care of a family. I was only seventeen. I was hardly capable of taking care of myself.

I had a friend, Kuddy, in the village. His family lived in a hut built from clay and coconut leaves. It was tiny, with not much more than a small firepit for cooking and a meagre space for eating. At night the same space was cleared for sleeping. Whenever the weather cooperated, Kuddy slept outside on the veranda with his dog. They were very poor, not like us. That is, not like we *had been*.

I found myself hanging out with Kuddy more and more. Often, I would ingratiate myself in order to sleep over. Kuddy's mother never objected. In the morning she would prepare string hoppers (handmade noodles) and sambal. Kindly, she would serve me first. She would often set aside extra food for when I visited, knowing that we did not have much. They gave me vegetables from their garden to take home. Occasionally, late at night, Kuddy and I would sneak into the neighbours' gardens and steal bananas and cassava. I knew stealing was wrong, but I couldn't help it; I had no choice but to feed my family and keep them alive.

My father was angry a lot at this time, and often his anger was directed at my mother. He yelled at her often, over the smallest things, but she never spoke back in anger. It was not her way. She would lower her head meekly, obediently, her eyes downcast. It made me furious. I felt so helpless!

For all his past faults, my father had been a generous provider. And not just for us: he had been incredibly generous to his large extended family, too. It was for this reason that I resented so deeply how the family turned its back on us now. The money was all gone. We had nothing. And they would not help. It was like he was dead to them.

I was angry all the time. Looking back on it now, I suppose it is possible that my father had abused his position over the years. He had humiliated my mother by bringing his sister-in-law into her house to share his bed. Who knows what else he had done?

Our situation was so dire at one point that my father began to tear down our house in order to sell the parts at the market for scrap. Glass doors, tiles from the roof, even locks.

I was having an increasingly difficult time dealing with the memories of being molested by the soldier on the train. I had no one I could talk to about it. The shame was eating me alive. Unlike Lathy, who had run away, I realized I could not run away from the memories that were haunting me. I was angry and depressed, and it occurred to me that joining the LTTE — the most popular rebel group — might sate my intense need for revenge. Joining the rebels could be empowering. I relished the idea of taking revenge on the bastard who had molested me, of taking my revenge on the Sinhalese majority who had ruined my family and were trying to destroy my people. Perhaps, I thought, there were more victims like me who were afraid to speak out. What if they molested or raped my sisters, too? I was determined to do something about it.

I had a childhood friend from Chavakachcheri Hindu College elementary school who was a member of LTTE, and one day I asked him to help me sign up.

He refused. "No, joining LTTE is not that simple. I don't want to get involved."

I was stunned and, frankly, heartbroken. "No," I pleaded, "you must introduce me. It is very important. You don't understand." I wanted to confess to him about the soldier who had molested me, but I couldn't. Anyway, I persisted for days, and about a week later he relented.

"Someone will come to you in a few days," he said.

"Who?" I asked.

"That is all you need to know."

A week went by and no one tried to contact me. I was very disappointed. I wondered what the LTTE had heard about my father and if they had decided I was an unacceptable risk because of him. Although my father never talked about politics, his friends were policemen, judges, and prominent businesspeople. He was a member of the Lions Club and knew a lot of Sinhalese officials. I guessed the LTTE knew about his background.

After sunset, I would often bike to hang out with my friends. One evening — it would have been in June 1984 — I went to the Thiyaku stores nearby and waited for my friends.

A young man of about twenty approached me. "Are you Logathasan?" he asked.

"Yes, I am. Who are you?"

"LTTE meeting today. Follow me."

I got on my bike and followed him. He led me to a hut surrounded by trees and bushes in a rundown section of town. "Inside," he said.

I left the bike by a tree and went inside the hut. It was dark. The only light came from a small kerosene lamp in the middle of the room. About twenty boys, mostly my age or a bit younger, were sitting on one side, and a man and his two bodyguards were sitting on the opposite side.

The man, who I assumed was the leader, was around thirty years old, stocky and muscular. He was wearing a dark short-sleeved shirt and dark trousers. He wasn't wearing a uniform, but he was holding a pistol in his right hand. A tiny capsule tied to a thread was hanging around his neck; later I learned that it was cyanide.

The two guards standing next to him were holding AK-47 assault rifles. They didn't look much older than me, but they seemed older. I guess it was the guns. They seemed very proud.

Everyone was quiet.

"Vanakkam!" the leader announced at last. *Greetings!*

It was a recruiting event. He spoke about our country, what was happening to Tamil people, and what we must all do to protect the Tamils from extinction by the government. He talked about the LTTE's accomplishments. At the end of the meeting, the leader demonstrated how to use his pistol and asked us to try handling it ourselves.

I was enchanted. I had never held a gun before, and I have to admit it was very empowering. The leader showed me how to load the bullets and change the magazine. Then he showed me how to point and shoot. I felt like James Bond. The gun was agreeably heavy with a pleasant heft. I could feel its power and strength and suddenly, I felt powerful and strong, too. The soldier from the train station entered my mind, and I thought about how satisfying it would be to put the end of the pistol to his forehead and pull the trigger.

I went home that night happier than I had been in years.

A few days later, I was approached on the street by another young man, whom I recognized from temple. His name was Ravi. I had come to know him fairly well and he was always very pleasant, but he hadn't seemed like the kind of person who would join the rebels. Plus, he had been born with a disability. I thought it odd that the LTTE would recruit people with disabilities as guerillas. Perhaps as long as one could pull a trigger, that was sufficient.

Ravi sensed my confusion. "The LTTE is not just about fighting with guns," he said. "We must also fight with words. In fact, words can be even more effective than bullets in our fight."

"I don't understand," I said. "When do I get a gun? I want to kill the soldiers."

He shook his head at my naïveté and smiled. "It has been decided that your talents are better suited to tasks other than fighting with guns."

My disappointment must have been obvious, because he nodded knowingly. "Everyone wants to fight with guns," Ravi admitted. "It's natural. We want to train you in the propaganda area."

"What about in the combat-training area?"

"No. It has been decided." He was becoming annoyed with me. "Besides, your father would never permit it. Your family is still very well known. It would be too risky for you — and for us."

My elation dissipated at the mention of my father. Dreams of avenging the soldier's attack on me vanished. I was furious at my father but cooled down after a time.

"I want to help in any way I can."

Ravi smiled and clapped me on the back. "Good man. We'll get started right away. And welcome to the cause!"

After that, we met often, usually three or four times a week, and almost always late at night. We mainly talked about the plans for the next day or two. In my case, that meant plans for distributing notices, taking up collections, or coming up with ideas for donations. It was fun being part of a group dedicated to such a worthwhile cause — but I was also aware that part of the appeal was doing something I knew my father would disapprove of.

The meetings lasted a long time, and often I would not return home until two or three in the morning. My father was always irate when I got home late, and he would yell at me. But I kept going. I didn't care what he thought. He had no idea I was meeting with the rebels. He must have thought

I was out with my friends, chasing girls or something. I liked that I had this secret from him. It made me feel independent.

One night, a young man showed up at my house saying that Ravi had sent him to me because he needed a place to sleep that night. He was wearing a sleeveless shirt and a sarong. He carried a large bag on his shoulder. I said he could stay with me in my brother Lathy's room. He didn't talk much. Not at all, in fact. He was constantly listening to a pocket radio that he kept at low volume.

Eventually I fell asleep.

In the middle of the night, my father burst into the room. He was enraged. He picked up the boy's bag and threw it outside. "Leave my house now!" he roared. The bag landed in the yard and its contents tumbled out: guns and hand grenades.

I yelled at my father. "What are you doing? He is my friend!"

The rebel rushed outside and gathered up the weapons, shoved them back into the bag, and ran off down the street. I ran after him, but he disappeared down a side street and I lost him.

Back at the house, my father was volcanic with anger. He screamed at me. "What are you doing with rebels? Do you want to be killed? Do you want your brother killed? Do you know what will happen to your mother and sisters if the police find out you are associating with rebels?" I thought he would kill me.

My mother had no idea what was going on but intervened anyway. My father was yelling, I was yelling, and my mother was in between, screaming for us to both stop yelling. Somehow, she calmed him down. Frankly, I did not care about his anger or what it would be like for him or the family. And what did he care about my mother? I was angry, too. I stormed back to my room and pretended to go to sleep.

Later, I snuck out and went to Ravi's house and told him what had happened. I stayed there that night.

My father hated the LTTE, but I loved belonging to a rebel group. It felt good. It wasn't the revenge I wanted, but it was all I had. Plus, most people supported the LTTE, especially after the Black July riots.

During my time with the LTTE, I was mostly tasked with distributing pamphlets and affixing posters to walls in public places like supermarkets, schools, and train stations. Occasionally, I solicited donations from the public. We would drive a tractor-trailer to collect coconuts and sell them to make money. People gave us food and drinks during these times.

Sometimes I wished I was playing a more active role with the rebels, as distributing leaflets and asking for small donations seemed a bit removed from the real action — too administrative. Still, I enjoyed the camaraderie. Sometimes, from the donations, I would bring rice, coconuts, sugar, and tea to my family.

And it wasn't like I was doing nothing. I had taken a stand. I was fighting for Tamil freedom and independence. It made me feel more secure to know that if the army conducted a surprise roundup, I could escape and hide out with my rebel friends.

It didn't last.

One night, during the curfew, I was told to stick notices on the walls around town. I was riding a motorbike with another recruit on the Kandy–Jaffna Highway. We usually slapped up posters at night; it was safer, as we didn't have to worry about anyone seeing us and betraying our activities. We rode through the silent, unlit neighbourhood. The street lights were turned off during curfews.

All of a sudden, we were caught in twin spears of bright light. I cursed. *Soldiers!*

I glanced behind us. A string of military trucks was parked along the shoulder of the highway, waiting in the dark for anyone violating the curfew. Immediately, I heard soldiers shouting and trucks roaring to life.

"They've spotted us!" my companion shouted to me. "Faster! Step on it!"

We unloaded on the throttle and raced off as fast as the motorcycle could manage. But there was no way we could outrun a military vehicle on our little motorcycle. The engine started sparking. I cursed again. "Probably overheated!" I yelled over my shoulder. I was nearing a junction, so I made a turn. "Hold on!"

We raced and bounced hard over the train tracks running parallel to the Kandy–Jaffna Highway and climbed a steep hill. The engine was on fire now. Just as we crested the hill, I swerved off the road and steered the bike into a high stand of brush. We flew off the bike and hit the ground with a dull, lung-clearing thump. The bike skidded, then wobbled drunkenly into the bush.

My companion started to moan, and I covered his mouth with my hand. "Quiet!" I hissed. We could hear the military trucks close behind us on the hill. We scrambled and crawled deeper into the bushes. We held our breath.

We heard sudden sharp squeaking sounds: brakes. Voices. *They know we are here*, I thought. *This is it. We will be tortured or killed.*

I could see the truck on the side of the road. It was equipped with rotating headlights, bright beams of light sweeping back and forth. An armoured car with a mounted machine gun had pulled up behind the truck. I watched the gun turning left and right, then aiming directly at us. I had stopped breathing. *What are they waiting for? What happens when they find us? They will kill us.*

It seemed as if we waited an hour, but it could not have been more than ten minutes. Suddenly, we heard someone bark an order. The searchlights were turned off and the soldiers boarded the trucks and drove off toward Chavakachcheri town.

We waited until we could no longer hear the engines, and even then we emerged only reluctantly from the bush.

"I think we are okay," I said.

"They must have been worried it was an ambush," my companion said. "That is why they didn't look for us."

It took us a few minutes to find the motorbike in the dark. It was badly damaged and would not start. We would have to walk it back. We left it in my uncle's yard and went home.

After about six months, the monotony of distributing pamphlets and repeating Marxist slogans had quelled my youthful revolutionary fervour. It had become unbearably boring and dreary, and I couldn't see that I was making any difference whatsoever.

More distressing was that a dangerous and damaging power struggle had erupted between the LTTE and rival guerilla groups, in particular the People's Liberation Organization of Tamil Eelam, which was cannibalizing the independence movement from within. As an increasing number of innocent civilians were either displaced from their homes or killed by this internecine warfare, I began to lose faith. What was the point of fighting the majority Sinhalese if Tamil civilians had as much to fear from the forces of liberation? It just didn't make much sense to me. I was extremely committed to independence, but it was hard — impossible — to maintain a focus on the big picture when rebels spent more time fighting one another than the Sinhalese majority.

I was still tormented by memories: the soldiers sweeping through our village and chasing me by helicopter, and the soldier molesting me on the train home. Over time, though, my intense thirst for revenge, my desire to kill Sri Lankan soldiers and to make them pay for what they had done to me, had abated. How many soldiers would I have to kill to expunge the memory of what happened? One? Ten? A hundred? It seemed pointless.

There is no antidote to grief but time. Killing, in any case, was not the answer.

But what was?

CHAPTER 14

I couldn't stand watching my father's downfall. With him no longer providing for the family and Lathy not there to support us, this burden had fallen into my lap. More and more I felt the need to escape — from the war, from my memories, from the sight of my family and of my country falling apart.

Jeya, a school friend from St. John's College, told me that the German government was helping Tamils escape the civil war by providing food and shelter to refugees, even providing them with expedited citizenship and opportunities to make a fresh start. I asked him how he knew this.

"My uncle has helped a lot of Tamils emigrate to Germany," he said. "He will help you."

At the time I didn't even know where Germany was or anything else about it.

"Germany is a very rich country," Jeya told me. "Everyone has a job. They treat Tamils very well there. Not like here. You will be treated very well. Once I get my passport, I am planning to go there, too."

A fresh start sounded like redemption. I would go to Germany and find a good job and send money back to my family. All would be well. No more war. No more destruction. No one hating us because we were Tamil. They would welcome us! We could live in peace. I imagined a grand welcoming party at the airport and never being afraid again.

I asked Jeya how much it would cost.

He shrugged. "Twenty thousand Sri Lankan rupees."

Twenty thousand rupees! I was staggered. It might as well have been twenty million. I did not, however, hesitate. I would find the money. "Tell your uncle I will go to Germany."

I decided to say nothing of my decision to my family — especially not to my mother, since I was convinced she would never let me leave. She had lost one son to another country already, and I was sure she would not countenance losing another. However, I was faced with another problem: I had used all of my savings during the war to buy food and items my family needed to survive. Where could I find the money to go to Germany?

My friend Prabhu and I had grown up together, going to the same primary school in Sangkaththaanai. His mother was a teacher, and she knew me very well. Prabhu and I went to see his mother. He told her I had a favour to ask.

I told her what I had decided. She listened attentively and respectfully; she asked me a lot of questions. *Do I have my passport? Who is helping me go to Germany? Where would I live in Germany?* What she did not ask me was what my parents thought of my idea. She must have assumed that they either knew and approved, or she had decided fleeing Sri Lanka was the only viable option. She worried about Prabhu, too.

Finally, she agreed to lend me the twenty thousand rupees ($740 U.S.). I was bursting with joy. I promised her that I would pay her back as soon as I found work in Germany.

When I met up with Jeya and told him I had the money, he explained that the cost included airfare to Germany and a bonded passport. This meant that a guarantor would bond my passport so that I could travel to all countries with a valid visa. He took my money and my passport and sent them to his uncle, who lived in Colombo. He gave me his uncle's phone number and instructed me to pick up the ticket and passport in Colombo the following week.

I was thrilled that I would be leaving my old life behind and would have a chance to begin a new and better life in Germany. Just to be on the safe side, I reminded Jeya to keep my plan confidential and not tell anyone — most importantly my family. I was also concerned that if news of my plan leaked, the LTTE might prevent me from leaving the country. I had not yet formally broken off ties with the group, and I was worried they might interpret my flight to Germany as an act of betrayal or disloyalty.

A few months earlier, I had gone to the fish market, next to the main bus station, to buy food for my family. As I neared, people were screaming and running away from the bus station. I couldn't see any military trucks or soldiers. But I did see a man lying in a pool of blood, wearing a sign around his neck. It read "Traitor." The owner of a nearby tea shop told me that two men carrying AK-47s had shot the man in front of a crowd of people at the bus stop. Apparently, he had given information about LTTE to government officials. They had made it clear they would do the same to anyone who betrayed them.

I started spending more time at Prabhu's house. I don't think my mother at first suspected my imminent escape to Germany. But I think the more time I spent away from home, the more she wondered. We had never talked about my membership in the LTTE; I know she disapproved, but I think some part of her understood.

I stayed with Prabhu for a couple of days before my departure. We spent a good deal of our time huddled over maps of Sri Lanka, figuring out the best routes to Colombo and talking about the trip and about Germany and about what the future would be like. In many ways it was the longest week of my life, but before I knew it, the day of my departure had arrived.

During all this time, my travel plan had been a secret mission between Prabhu and me. But I could not keep my plan a secret forever. The night before my departure, I slept at home. Early the next morning, I found my mother washing dishes by the well. She looked very tired. I was overwhelmed by such a staggering wave of guilt that my legs buckled. She looked up from the dishes, saw me, and smiled.

I gave her a hug, and she looked at me sharply. "What is it?"

My throat was as dry as dust. "Amma," I announced, "I am leaving." At first, I was not sure she had heard me. She betrayed no emotion. "Amma, I am going to Colombo today. From there I am going Germany. I will find work. I will send money for you."

Her hands flew to her face and she began wailing in a voice that sounded deeply frightened. She was hitting her head with her hands, yelling, "It is too dangerous. The Sinhalese will kill you. You are only eighteen years old. Please don't go."

"I have to, Amma. It is the only way I can help the family."

She refused to listen. "No!" she said. "If you go, I will kill myself."

It is rather common in Tamil culture for one to threaten to kill oneself to trigger sympathy. It almost worked.

"Amma," I pleaded at last, "I have no choice. We have nothing. I must go to Germany and find a good job and send money home. One day we will all be together. You will see. I promise."

I assured her that I would be okay and that I would write to her when I reached Germany. Finally, she seemed to sense that my stubbornness was genuine and that nothing would change my mind.

I would like to say that I regretted my decision to leave, but the truth is that I was restless and anxious to go. My mother, however, was inconsolable.

I had about a thousand rupees in travel money. Before I left, my mother insisted on stitching a hidden pocket in my underwear to keep my money safe. She wept as she sewed. After I had changed, I packed a small bag with a second pair of trousers, a sweater, and a pair of slippers. She made me tea, and we sat on the kitchen floor in awkward silence as I gulped it down. Then I picked up my bag and started to walk toward the front gate.

"Wait!" she called. She ran inside the house and brought back a picture. It was the Lord Shiva and Parvati, the sacred Hindu god and goddess. "Keep it wherever you go," she said. "They will protect you."

I still have that picture. I have kept it with me to this very day.

"Will you not say goodbye to your father?" she asked.

I shook my head and resumed walking. She followed me for a few steps, but I did not stop or turn around. I suddenly thought about what my father might do after I was gone. *Will he beat her? Will he mistreat my sisters and brother? Who will take care of them?*

I hesitated. The guilt was almost overwhelming as I opened the gate, but I kept walking. Home was already a memory.

Massive bombing campaigns by the Sri Lankan security forces and the LTTE had destroyed most of the roads and railway tracks in the Northern Province. As a result, the closest functioning train station was in Kilinochchi, a town about forty miles to the south. The once-per-week train bound for Colombo was scheduled to depart from the station at noon.

It was about seven when I left our family house. There was no chance of catching a bus or train from Chavakachcheri to Kilinochchi, and walking the distance would take me about eleven hours. My only hope was hitching rides from passing cars, which — with a great deal of luck — would take about an hour. I was determined to get there before noon.

There were no cars, so I ran along the side of the road until a van came along. I frantically gestured at them to stop, and thankfully, they did. It was a relief — and so much faster — to sit instead of having to run! However, the ride was very short.

At the Kandy–Jaffna Highway, I got a ride from a Thaddi van (a grocery truck) to Kodikamam. Then I ran all the way to Mirusuvil. Just outside Mirusuvil, I waved to a motorcycle.

The rider stopped and asked, "Where are you going?"

"To Kilinochchi railway station," I replied.

"I am going to Palai," he said. "Hop on."

I jumped on the back of the motorcycle and we tore off down the road.

We soon arrived at Palai and, unfortunately, I had to start jogging again. Not long after, however, I spotted a minibus on its way to Paranthan. I waved it to a stop and hopped on.

Along the way, we had to divert around massive holes that pockmarked the roads — craters from exploded bombs. Military vehicles, many belching smoke and littered with bullet holes, were flipped upside down or had been run off the road. Dozens of trees had been amputated of limbs by bullets and mortar fire, and many had been felled and laid across the road as barriers to tanks and trucks.

Finally, I reached the train station in Kilinochchi. It had taken about four hours. Not bad! Men and women with bags and groceries were boarding the train, the Yal Devi (Queen of Jaffna). I hadn't a minute to spare. I approached the ticket counter with my fare.

The clerk looked at me. "Train is full," he announced. "Come back next week."

I was stunned; I had barely escaped my hometown and already I had hit a huge hurdle. I walked to the platform and saw that the train was not at all full. Why had the clerk told me it was?

I am not going back to my village, I told myself. But if I missed this train, where was I going to stay for a week? What would happen to my passport and my flight ticket?

I will sit on the roof of the train without a ticket if I have to!

I returned to the ticket counter. "I must get a ticket for the train," I said as I slid an extra ten rupees across the counter with my ticket fare. I was issued a ticket immediately.

Greatly relieved, but not happy about having to dip into my travel money already, I boarded the train. Immediately I was seized with fear. My heart began pounding and I had difficulty breathing. I could feel the soldier behind me, his hot, dank breath on my neck, and I could hear him laughing with his fellow soldiers about what he had done to me. The memory was so vivid I was nearly sick.

The train was not crowded. After a moment my panic eased and I managed to make my way down the aisle to a seat near an older couple. *No one will bother me if I sit near them*, I thought. Looking back, I am not sure exactly why I thought that; I doubt they would have been any help at all if there had been a problem.

A few minutes later, the train lurched forward and started down the track out of the station. It took about an hour and a half to reach Vavuniya railway station. There were many military checkpoints along the way. Soldiers with submachine guns would get on the train and randomly ask for identification. They ordered some men to get out of the train for questioning. I never saw those men get back on the train.

A couple of seats away, I noticed a girl who, I thought, looked like she might be from Colombo. She had boarded the train in Kilinochchi, so I assumed she was Tamil. She wasn't wearing any pottu — a red dot would have meant that she was married and black dot that she was single — likely to hide her identity as a Tamil. She approached me and introduced herself. Her name was Devi. She asked where I was headed.

I was shocked at how forward she was. But happy. Usually, local girls were quiet and shy. Out of respect, they generally wouldn't even talk to their elders or relatives in public. "Colombo," I said.

"I studied in Colombo," she said, smiling. "That's where I've lived most of my life." She turned and walked back to her seat.

About an hour later she came by again. Devi turned out to be an accomplished talker. I was both confused and excited by her forwardness. She was a bit older than I was, and she said she was travelling with her father, her mother, and a younger brother. She asked me about the nature of my trip.

I briefed her on my plans.

She smiled. She, too, was travelling to Europe. "I am going to France to live with my uncle," she said. After the Black July riots, large numbers of Tamils were leaving Sri Lanka and moving to other countries. "I plan to study in France," she said. "There is a better future there."

We chatted for a while, then she went back and sat with her family.

As the train approached the city, the landscape transformed. The green empty fields that stretched to the horizon were replaced by cars, concrete highways and roads, tall buildings that created their own sawtoothed horizon, stores and shops crowded together, and houses stacked close like a dense forest.

Colombo was the first real city I had ever seen up close, and compared to our tiny village, it was enormous. I could hardly believe my eyes. The city was much more modern than our village, which was mostly farmland with little huts made of clay and coconut leaves; there were only a handful of houses with cement walls and tiled roofs in Sangkaththaanai.

It was dusk by the time the train pulled into the station. The city was busy, with people scurrying everywhere like an army of ants. I was tired and hungry but enormously relieved that I had made it to Colombo with only a minimum amount of trouble. The next step was to get my passport and ticket. Then I would be on my way to Germany.

The minute I left the station, I began looking for accommodations for the night. Tensions between Tamils and Sinhalese were at an all-time high in 1985, and the majority of the population in Colombo was Sinhalese. It was not safe for Tamils. It was common for Tamils to be attacked in Colombo, especially by gangs or thieves. And since I did not speak Sinhala, I decided to avoid cheap hotels or hostels where I might be discovered. I figured I would be safest in a mosque. At that time, Muslims — a small percentage of the population — were neutral and tended to be left alone by both Hindu Tamils and Buddhist Sinhalese.

After walking for thirty minutes or so, I found a mosque. I knocked on the door. A young man peeked through a little window, then opened the door. I told him that I was from the North and asked if I could sleep inside for the night. We spoke in Tamil, of course. He graciously invited me to spend the night but insisted that I leave the premises before sunrise. If the Sinhalese discovered that a Tamil was staying there, he insisted, the mosque would be burned down in retribution. He offered me tea and showed me a corner in the mosque where I could sleep. I was hungry. All I had that day were a Necto soda and peanuts on the train. But I was too grateful to have found a safe place to sleep to care about being hungry.

I thanked him and settled down on the cement floor for the night, using my bag as a pillow. It was very quiet, and before long I fell fast asleep. Still, I woke up occasionally and checked my secret pocket to make sure my money was safe. I thought about my mother and about my sisters and brother. I wondered if my siblings were waiting for me to come home or if my mother had explained to them what I had done.

Mostly, however, I thought about Germany. *My new home.* How proud my mother and my family would be when I had earned enough money to bring them to Germany, too.

It will be our home then.

CHAPTER 15

I awoke to the sounds of the city: honking horns, rush-hour traffic roaring along the road, buses braking, pedestrians chattering on the streets as they walked to work. I approached the young cleric and thanked him for allowing me to sleep there despite the great risk to himself.

I left the mosque and walked to a phone booth to call the office where my friend's uncle would have my passport and ticket to Germany. Once I had them, I would be off to the airport. I dialed the number.

"This number is not in service."

That is odd, I said to myself, not too concerned. *I must have made a mistake.* I consulted the phone number again and redialed.

"This number is not in service."

I stared at the phone, confused. I dialed a few more times but kept hearing the same recorded message. *What is happening? Why isn't Jeya's uncle answering the phone?* It made no sense.

Okay, I thought. *Think. What should I do now? There has to be a reasonable explanation. It's fine. Not to worry.*

I thought it through. First, there were no phones in Sangkaththaanai and therefore no way of getting in touch with Jeya to confirm his uncle's number. Second, I only had the uncle's number and not his address. Third, I didn't speak Sinhala and I was utterly alone in a strange city in the middle of a civil war where I was the enemy. Suddenly my brain was running at a million miles an hour. *If the Sinhalese find out I am Tamil, I will be robbed, beaten, or even killed.*

I decided to look for my friend Nishan, who was living in Anderson Flats, an area of Colombo where a lot of middle-class Tamil families lived. When I got there, however, it was a ghost town. Burned-out cars and vans sat on the side of the roads. After the Black July riots, the Tamils had fled, and it seemed no one had returned. The neighbourhood was completely abandoned.

I wandered the city with no destination in mind other than a travel agent, who might be able to help me out. I must have walked for hours before my feet gave out and I flagged a bus and climbed aboard.

"Oba koheda yanne?"

I had no idea what he was saying, but I guessed he was asking my destination so that he could issue a ticket. I was scared of speaking Tamil, though, and instead pretended I was mute; I signed that I couldn't talk and exited the bus at the next stop.

I walked for a long time in the streets and alleys. The city was busy and crowded with people. I was famished, and the aroma of food from restaurants made my mouth water, but I decided not to spend any of my limited amount of money until I had received my passport and flight ticket. Remembering the discipline at boarding school, I put my self-control to the test.

Sunset was approaching when I saw a crowd of people walking and clapping. I went over to find out what was going on. Galle Face Beach in Colombo was a well-known area for street performers. One performer bent backwards and inserted a slender two-foot-long sword into his throat and then withdrew it again with no harm done! Another swallowed gasoline, lit his mouth with a cigarette lighter, and spat out flames. The audience seemed very impressed, and the performers circled the crowd after each act, soliciting tips.

Other performers, however, were beggars. Many were missing limbs or suffered from other deformities — one man was blind — and obviously had no means for making a living other than doing tricks. One man with no legs simply dragged himself along the ground, begging. No one applauded and most of the crowd acted embarrassed and ignored him.

The sunset was magnificent: bright orange and red lit the sky like fire.

By now I was incredibly tired and decided to find a secluded place on the beach to sleep for the night. As I had the night before, I used my bag as a pillow, curling up in the warm, soft sand. Once I had made sure my money was still securely tucked away, I allowed myself to relax and lie on my back staring up into the sky, counting stars. I hadn't eaten yet, but, frankly, fear and worry consumed me so much that hunger was not even on my mind. I was exhausted and fell asleep immediately.

Again, the noise of rush-hour traffic startled me awake.

Three days had elapsed since I had left home and I hadn't eaten any more than those peanuts from the train. My stomach ached from lack of food. I had drunk only water from the taps on the streets. I felt dizzy and weak.

I was feeling desperate. I was downcast and discouraged. As much as I did not want to admit it, I realized that I had been cheated by Jeya's uncle. To be betrayed by a fellow Tamil was difficult to accept. What I needed was a person I could trust. But who? I had no relatives in Colombo. And there was no way I could trust a stranger. Colombo had been the epicentre of the Black July riots. What was I to do?

With no real plan, I ended up walking the streets, first in one direction and then in another, not really knowing where I was headed or why or what I hoped to accomplish. I went to hang out in Gangaramaya Park near Galle Face Beach, where there were plenty of trees to keep me cool during the heat of the day.

By sundown I had lost hope. I went back to the same spot on the beach and fell into a troubled sleep. The bright twinkling stars seemed to mock my cloudy disposition. I thought about school, my home in Sangkaththaanai, my cousins and friends, my brothers and sisters, my mother. *So far away*, the stars seemed to be telling me.

I thought, too, of the soldier on the train. I thought of my dream of a new life in a place called Germany. A new life for me and for my family.

So far away.

I woke up more exhausted than when I went to sleep. I felt as stiff as a board and my stomach was tied up in knots. I was desperately hungry. I had not washed in four days, and I smelled. My hair was a mess. My clothes were wrinkled and dirty. I washed myself as best I could in the ocean, and while I dried myself off in the early morning sunshine, I thought about what I would do that day.

I took the picture my mother had given me from my bag. "Lord Shiva and Parvati," I prayed, "I need your help."

Once again I wandered the streets, without aim or purpose. I hung out at a park, looking for Tamil people who might help me. Colombo was so different than anything I had ever experienced. I finally understood the expression *a fish out of water*.

In my village, Tamil men always wore the thiruneeru and women put the pottu on their forehead and fresh flowers in their hair. The air was infused with the scent of jasmine flowers every morning, and the temple bells rang with the sound of peace and serenity. Families would go in groups to the temples or to the movies.

But the men and women I came upon in Colombo were different. They always seemed to be in a hurry. None of the men wore the thiruneeru, nor the women the pottu. *Perhaps, I thought, some of them are Tamils who are afraid.* The people I saw wore dresses, trousers, and shirts instead of traditional Tamil clothes like saris and sarong.

I wandered the streets as I had the day before, hoping to stumble upon someone or something that might help. I came upon a plaza in what seemed a nicer part of Colombo and on a whim decided to enter. It seemed like the kind of place that might have a travel agency.

It was becoming painfully clear that I had not been very resourceful up to that point. My plans had been haphazard at best. All my life, I had been an act-first-and-think-second type of person, but now my situation was truly desperate.

On my way through the plaza, I bumped into someone and muttered a hasty apology. Too late, I realized I had spoken in Tamil. I was seized with terror. Had I given myself away?

"Logathasan? Is that you?"

My terror turned suddenly to confusion. I stared at the young woman standing in front of me. She was smiling.

"Devi?" I could not believe my eyes! It was the young woman from the train.

She nodded and burst out laughing. "What are you doing here?"

I made a shushing gesture, my finger to my lips, and in a low voice I explained that I was terrified that I might be discovered to be a Tamil and beaten or killed. I might put her in danger as well.

She agreed and gestured with her head for me to follow her. We went to a quiet place off the main road and made sure no one was around or within eavesdropping distance. "What happened to you? You don't look good at all!"

I told her my story of how I'd been swindled. "So now I have no passport and no ticket to Germany."

She was mortified and angry to learn that a fellow Tamil had cheated me. "Another Tamil did this to you!" she said furiously. "Shameful! Come with me."

Since Devi lived in Colombo, she had grown up speaking Sinhala. And she likely had more experience dealing with Sinhalese than I did. She seemed confident, anyway; I was a nervous wreck. She grabbed me by the hand and practically frog-marched me to an office about five minutes away. Along the way, she asked me about what happened.

"Who is this Andrew?"

I explained that he was Jeya's uncle.

She asked me who I gave the money and passport to.

"I gave it to Jeya and he transferred the money and sent the passport to his uncle."

"When are you supposed to pick up the ticket?"

"This week," I said. "But the number I have is not in service."

She frowned and nodded. "Give me the number."

I must have looked completely confused. She explained. "Much of the business in Colombo operates ... under the table. Do you understand?"

"No."

She smiled. "Never mind. It doesn't matter. I will see what I can do."

She made a few phone calls while I patiently sat there. It only took a few minutes. "Meet me here tomorrow, ten o'clock" she said. "I have to go."

I walked back to the beach, where I felt safe and blended in with the beggars, performers, and spectators. I continued to act like I was mute and avoided speaking to anyone. I was starving and weak, but I was no longer hopeless. I believed Devi would help me. I decided my priority had to be making myself stronger for my trip to Germany. I found a cheap street vendor and bought rice and two curry dishes for ten rupees (thirty-seven U.S. cents). The food was folded in banana leaves and wrapped in a piece of newspaper. The rice and curry warmed up the banana leaves, creating a pleasant, almost intoxicating aroma. I was so hungry

I was drooling as I unwrapped the newspaper and folded back the banana leaves.

I ate as slowly as I could, meaning to savour each and every tiny bite, but it was no use; I gulped down half the meal very quickly. I did manage to stop, though, and forced myself to save the rest for later despite my hunger. Already, I could feel my spirits lifting. I felt warm inside and stronger.

I placed the remaining half of my meal inside my bag and resolved to eat no more until bedtime. For the rest of the day I wandered the streets but now more as a tourist would. I told myself that by the next day, I would be on my way to Germany and a new life. Even though Colombo was almost as exotic and unfamiliar to me as Germany, it represented my old life and I wanted to enjoy it as much as I could before I left.

That night I went back to the beach and, after enjoying the rest of my rice and curry feast, went to sleep happy and excited.

The next morning, I awoke early, even before the cars and buses, and bathed in the Indian Ocean, then let the sun's rays dry my body. I was impatient and anxious, but when the time came, I walked back to our meeting place and waited for Devi. A car pulled over next to me, and the driver asked me to get inside. Devi waved from the back seat. There was a man in the car, and he waved to me in greeting as well. I jumped in and we drove off.

Devi did not introduce her companion, and I decided I would just sit in the car and keep my mouth shut. He was tall and very dark. He wore a short-sleeved shirt and dark trousers and looked very serious. He and Devi were speaking in Sinhala, and I assumed he was Sinhalese. I had no choice but to trust Devi.

The car seemed rather new and luxurious. I assumed Devi's family was very wealthy. She also seemed to have a lot of connections.

Devi and her companion were talking animatedly. She seemed fired up about something. Yet my stomach was churning because of my fear of the unknown.

About a half-hour later, the car pulled up suddenly in front of a small hotel. The driver and Devi's companion exited the car quickly and ran inside.

"What is going on?" I asked.

Devi didn't answer me. A minute or two later she threw open the car door and jumped out.

"Come with me," she commanded.

I got out of the car and followed her.

In the hallway the driver and Devi's companion were banging on a door. A man opened the door. He was very tall, clean-shaven, and dressed in a smart suit and tie.

"Gaman balapatra saha mudal koheda?" Devi's companion yelled in Sinhala.

The man looked confused.

"Paspottum kasum enke?" Devi also shouted in Tamil. *Where is the passport and money?*

The man suddenly looked very scared. I think he had expected the person knocking at the door to be his driver. He had a small piece of luggage at his side. The two men were yelling at him in Sinhala. I didn't know what they were saying, but the man put his hand up and sat down on his bed. They continued to argue for about five minutes.

Devi explained to me that the man sitting on the bed was Jeya's uncle, Andrew, and that he had sold my passport to someone else. However, she said, he had been convinced by the driver and Devi's companion to return my money.

I was badly shaken. "Without my passport, how can I go to Germany?"

Devi was furious that a Tamil had robbed another Tamil. "You are despicable! You are worse than a thief!" she told him.

Andrew finally agreed to make some calls. On the phone, he was talking vigorously, and his tone seemed to swing from angry to solicitous. Finally, after about fifteen minutes, he told us that he had some good news. He had found the passport.

"Where is it?" asked Devi.

He told her the address and Devi instructed the driver to pick it up and come right back. Meanwhile, Andrew wrote a cheque for twenty thousand rupees and handed it to Devi.

"Thank you," Devi said.

Andrew did not look pleased.

Devi told her companion to stay with Andrew and me while she went to the bank to cash the cheque. Andrew did not apologize to me, and he hardly looked at me. He just sat on the bed and stared at the ceiling. If he felt any remorse at all for his theft, he didn't show it. I guess this is what life was like for some. I realized how naive I had been.

When Devi returned with my twenty thousand rupees, I was overjoyed. I thanked her over and over. Still, I was wracked with worry. What if the driver never returned?

A few hours later, however, the driver returned with my passport. Unbelievable!

I thanked Devi and she said not to worry. Then she said that she had to leave because she was moving to France the following day and needed to pack. And just like that, she left.

One of my true regrets in life is that I was too stunned by all that was happening, I forgot to ask Devi for her contact details. I never had a chance to thank her for her selflessness.

She had only met me briefly once in a train, but in a very real sense she saved my life. I only hope that someday she might read this and realize how grateful I am to her.

Back at the beach that night, I slept fitfully. It seemed every fifteen minutes I startled myself awake to check that my passport and money were secure. For most of the night I slept on my back with my hand over my pocket, where I had tucked my passport.

The next day, I was set to buy my ticket at the travel agency when the agent informed me that I needed a sponsor to bond my passport. The agent understood Tamil and could explain the requirement to me. It sounded very complicated, and I had no idea how in the world I could find someone authorized to be my sponsor. I was devastated. What was I supposed to do? I knew not one soul in Colombo except Devi, and I had no idea where she lived. And anyway, she was on her way to France.

Once again, I felt my plans collapsing. How was I going to find a sponsor in a city where I was not only a stranger but a despised Tamil who feared for his life? And even if I could find someone to bond my passport, it would cost me a fortune — maybe more than I had. My sky-high hopes crashed headlong into a black despair.

Then I remembered Jeya had once told me that his sister worked at the Bank of Ceylon in Colombo. Perhaps she could help me! When I was fourteen years old, I had visited Jeya and his family during the summer holidays. I didn't remember the address, but I knew that they lived in a town very close to Colombo called Mattakkuliya.

I started walking. It turned out to be about a two-hour walk from Galle Face Beach.

Mattakkuliya was not as prosperous as I remembered it from my first visit. Many of the nicer buildings now looked abandoned or dilapidated, and some had burned down. It had once been a very busy area, but it was now rundown and mostly empty. Garbage was strewn everywhere.

I managed to find Jeya's family's home. The front part of the roof was burned, and some parts had fallen to the ground. However, their house looked intact. I hesitated at first, then decided to knock on the door. A young lady opened it, and I told her that I was looking for Jeya's sister.

"I am his sister," she said. "Nalini."

I didn't recognize her at first, but she recognized me and smiled. She told me to come inside before anyone saw us.

Nalini told me more about the Black July riots of a year and a half before. Gangs of thugs had burned down the Tamil houses and shops and beaten up any Tamils they could find. "Many were killed with machetes like animals," she said. She told me she was petrified to live there.

I asked her why she stayed.

She stared into the distance and shrugged. "It is my home."

"I have no intention to stay and be killed with a machete," I said.

"No," she agreed. "Boys and men are targets. You are not safe. But it is not safe for girls or women, either."

I had heard stories about thugs hunting down and raping women. I quickly changed the subject and told her about my situation.

"I work at the bank," she said. "I am respected there." She volunteered to sponsor my bond.

I was elated.

She told me that sponsors are allowed to sponsor only two people during their lifetime. She had used one already, and she said she had been saving the other for Jeya. "But I think he will stay," she said. "I want you to have it."

I thanked her profusely and offered her one thousand rupees (thirty-seven U.S. dollars), but she refused.

She explained to me that it would take about a week for the passport to be bonded. "Go to the passport office and check back then."

I thanked her again for her kindness and gave her my passport. I trusted her. I still trusted Jeya, too. He had been a very good friend to me, and I didn't believe he had any idea that his uncle was untrustworthy. Still, after the trouble I'd had retrieving my passport, I had a sudden moment of doubt after handing it over. Once again I was stateless.

"I would offer for you to stay here," she said apologetically, "but it is too dangerous." Living alone as a woman was not ideal, but it was safer than having a rebel-aged male in the house.

I did not relish the idea of spending another week sleeping on the beach, and she seemed to intuit my disappointment. "I know a family that will take you in," she said. "It is not far away. In Mattakkuliya. The woman is Muslim. She is very kind, and I will talk to her. Don't worry. You will be safe. Here is her address. Go to her later tonight."

I was so grateful to Nalini, and any doubts I had about being able to trust her disappeared.

The Muslim family had a tiny house inside an alley so narrow that it could only be reached by foot. There were no streetlights, so at night people walked with kerosene lamps. Before the riots, Tamils had lived there, too. But since then, they had all fled. Only Muslims lived there now.

When I knocked on the door, a woman answered and greeted me.

I told her my name. "Nalini sent me."

She brightened. "Vanakkam!" she said. "Please, come in."

She said I was welcome to stay in a storage area at the back. "It isn't much," she said, "but it will keep the rain off."

The woman was in her early thirties and quite short — less than five feet tall. She wore a half-sari that also covered her head. I thanked her profusely. "It's a palace compared to where I've been sleeping," I said. I told her my story.

She nodded and said she understood. I was very welcome to share her home, she said, but she had a few house rules. First, I must leave the house before sunrise. Second, I could come back after sunset but not before. "Too dangerous!" she said.

It was my turn to say that I understood.

She had a son and a daughter, she told me, aged ten and twelve. "They will not bother you."

I smiled and told her about my brothers and sisters.

Every morning during my time in Mattakkuliya, I was awakened early — usually by one of the children, who seemed both very shy of me and familiar. They gave me tea and fresh-baked bread for breakfast. Before the sun was up, I would start wandering the city. It was odd how quickly I learned how to amuse myself in a big city by doing absolutely nothing. I walked, looked in store windows, sat in parks and people-watched, hung out at the beach — basically lived a life of leisure. Usually I skipped eating during the day. It was cheaper that way, and I thought that any interaction with the Sinhalese, even with the street vendors, could be dangerous.

Shortly after sunset each day, I would find my way back to the house in Mattakkuliya. I looked forward to eating evening meals with the family; it wasn't something I was used to. The mother prepared the meals, and we all sat down together on the floor to eat. The prawn curry cooked in coconut milk and served with warm rice was delicious. I talked to them about my family, about life at boarding school. I also talked a lot about my plan to move to Germany. "I am going to be free," I told them. "I will have a good job, and I can pay to have my mother and siblings move to Germany, too. It will be a good life."

We also talked about the riots and about the hatred between Tamils and Sinhalese. The mother explained that the Qur'an forbids hatred. "We must take care of one another," she said. She sighed. "It does not always work out that way, however."

I agreed. I had never read the Qur'an and had no idea what it said, but I believed it to be true because she did. After all, she was sheltering a Tamil in her home.

I realized that I had seen no trace of her husband anywhere and that he was never mentioned. As I was living off her kindness and hospitality, I thought it disrespectful to inquire after him. Perhaps he had died. I don't know. At that time in Sri Lanka, Muslims were for the most part tolerated; over time that would change.

Her son and daughter often wandered into the storage area, and we would play together. They reminded me of my younger brother and sisters.

When the day I'd been waiting for finally arrived, I walked to the passport office, which was about two hours away. I showed the clerk my identity card and told him I had arrived to pick up my passport. He looked at my card and frowned. I think he realized from my name that I was Tamil. He opened a binder, looked at me, and said, "Next week"

I placed one hundred rupees ($3.70 U.S.) on the counter. "Can you check again?"

He closed the binder with the rupees inside. "Come back tomorrow."

The next day, I showed up at the same time. When I passed my identity card across the counter, the clerk passed me back my passport. I opened it quickly to make sure it had been bonded for all countries. I almost laughed aloud when I realized it had been officially processed two days ago. The clerk had told me to come back later just to get a bribe. But I didn't care at that point. I had my passport! I was truly on my way to Germany!

I was so excited I practically ran to the travel agency to book my flight to East Berlin the following day.

That night, I returned to Mattakkuliya for the last time.

The next day, I awoke, showered, and dressed. My Muslim mother very kindly had washed and ironed my clothes. I was packed and ready to go, and I said my goodbyes. It was very hard. She had taken me in, a complete stranger. I had stayed with this family for only ten days, but it had felt much longer.

As I was on my way out, she asked me to wait for her by the end of the alley. She couldn't risk having anyone see her and her children with me.

I didn't understand, but she smiled and I did as I was told. I watched her and her two children walk away. A few minutes later, she returned with her children. She waved for me to come. She had arranged for a rickshaw to take me to the airport!

"I will travel with you," she said. "I speak Sinhala. It will be safer that way. Less conspicuous. Come."

I said goodbye to the daughter, and the mother, her son, and I climbed into the rickshaw. I could not sit still and I kept turning my head left and right looking everywhere as we travelled to the airport. The rickshaw driver looked back at me a few times with what seemed to be a troubled look on his face. But I worried in vain, and we arrived safely at the airport. I tried to pay the woman for her kindness, but she refused. So I decided to gift my watch to her son. "A memento," I said, touching my hand to my chest, "for my Colombo family." Mother and son smiled at me.

With mixed emotions, I watched them drive away. The Muslim mother adored her children. She had photos of them everywhere in their tiny home. Before I left their home, I asked if I could keep one photograph of her children. I have lost touch with them, but the memories are still intact.

I was eager to begin my new life in Germany. But as I approached the airport doors, my mind was filled with the larger sadness of leaving my family and my homeland, possibly forever.

Colombo's Bandaranaike International Airport was crowded with travellers, and the military presence was immediately obvious. Everywhere I looked, I saw soldiers with submachine guns, many with dogs by theirs sides. My heart began pounding.

There had been a rumour that the LTTE was planning an attack on the airport in retaliation for the brutal attacks on

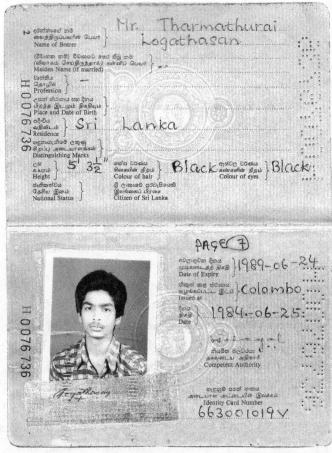

I wore the same shirt (shown in the passport) when I left Sri Lanka.

Tamils in the Black July riots. About a week earlier, the LTTE had bombed the northern railway line, Yal Devi, at Murikandy, killing thirty-four people, including twenty-two soldiers, and completely destroying the tracks. Tensions were very high.

I had put on the same shirt I was wearing in my passport photo, just in case, and I walked directly to the check-in counter and handed the clerk my passport and ticket. After inspecting my passport, he issued me a boarding pass. I had no luggage to check in, so I went straight to security. Despite my nervousness, I sailed through with surprising ease. Ironically, the government was actually encouraging Tamils to emigrate — the fewer Tamils the better, I suppose — so the military, in particular, was not disposed to create any barriers for Tamils leaving the country.

I will never forget buckling myself into my seat and waiting anxiously for the plane to finally lift off. It was my first time on an airplane, and I found the experience both terrifying and magical.

It was quite some time before I felt relaxed enough to loosen my death grip on the armrests. At last, I smiled. I had done it. I was free. I was headed to Germany! I started giggling. Then, just as quickly, it hit me: I was headed to Germany. I had no idea what I was doing. I knew not one word of German. I knew not a soul. I was on my own. My mouth turned very dry. *What am I doing?*

I had never been more scared in my life.

CHAPTER 16

When I was a little boy, I would watch the jets flying high in the sky and would run in the fields pretending that I was one. At Sangkaththaanai, not many planes flew over; I would wait for days just to see one.

And here I was on my first plane! How I wished I could tell my friend Prabhu what it was like.

My first stop would be a short layover in Moscow, and then I would transfer to a larger plane for a flight to East

Berlin, Germany. At the time, most commercial flights between Colombo and Europe were operated by the Russian airline Aeroflot. I was so new to the experience of flying that I didn't know what a layover was, or the difference between a direct flight and a commuter flight. More importantly, I had no idea that East Berlin and West Berlin were completely separate places. It would be a rather rude introduction to Cold War politics.

A few hours into the flight, I noticed the other passengers were staring at me. When I looked back at them, they looked away or at their magazines. *What are they looking at?* I wondered. When I looked up and down the aisle, I realized I was the only person of colour on the entire plane. Everyone else was white. This was another first for me. I had never seen so many white people in one place.

When the plane landed at Berlin Schönefeld Airport in East Berlin, I looked through the window and was puzzled. There was some kind of white powder blanketing the ground. *That must be snow!* I thought. And we seemed to be a long way from the terminal.

We were told that due to heavy snowfall, the aircraft had landed far away from the terminal and we would have to walk outside to a bus waiting to ferry us to the terminal. A staircase on wheels was rolled up to the side of the plane and the door was swung open. Passengers — most of them wrapped up tight in big jackets with fur collars — began climbing down the stairs.

I didn't have a jacket. All I had was a light sweater. I stepped out into the freezing cold air and jumped back into the plane like a startled terrier. Passengers behind me started laughing. Hunching up my shoulders against the stabbing cold, I followed the passengers ahead of me and climbed onto a bus.

Completely unfamiliar with airport procedures and protocol, I zombie-walked behind the crowd headed to immigration, where my passport was stamped. Again, I fell into line behind the flow of the crowd and found myself boarding a train, not at all sure where it was headed. When the train stopped at the next station, two policemen boarded. They were wearing blue uniforms and hats. Each had a baton at their waist and a gun on the other hip. One officer was holding the leash of a dog. The only person of colour on the train, I must have stood out like a sore thumb, because they headed straight toward me.

"*Reisepass!*" one barked at me in German.

I saw passengers handing over their passports, so I did the same. The officers studied it intently, occasionally looking up and staring at me and then looking back at the passport.

"*Kommen Sie mit uns! Oben! Jetzt!*"

I had no idea what he wanted, but I noticed other passengers on the train were looking at me with startled expressions.

"I do not speak —" I tried to explain in Tamil.

"*Oben! Jetzt!*" The officer looked angry and impatient with my confusion. The dog tugged on its leash, snarling.

I stood up and attempted to convey through hand gestures that I was anxious to comply. The policeman jerked his head to the side, indicating I was being ordered to exit the train. I stepped into the aisle, so terrified I was shaking, and with one policeman in front and one behind, I got off the train. On the platform I was directed to follow them through the station to a van that was parked at the curb.

"*Innerhalb!*"

I kept repeating "Germany! Germany!" at them but to no avail.

They hoisted me into the van by the shoulders and slammed the door shut. I heard the clinking of a lock. Hard benches ran the length of the van on either side and I sat down. I was alone. It was very cold inside the van and I could not stop shivering. My shaking was so intense my joints ached.

About a half-hour later, we arrived at an underground police station. One officer got out of the van and signalled for me to get out. Another officer took my bag and indicated that I was to follow them. Once again, I walked between the two officers. I was moving freely — I wasn't handcuffed — but they had kept my passport.

I was led inside the building and down a nondescript corridor with cement walls and doors — doors with iron bars — on either side. I was too scared to ask the officers what was happening, but even as an inexperienced traveller, I knew this was not normal. One of the officers unlocked a door, put me inside, and locked the door behind me.

My passport was not returned.

The cell had a sink, a toilet, and a cement bench cantilevered from the wall. The bench had a dual purpose; it could be used as a seat or a bed. The cell was no more than five feet wide and ten feet deep. There were no windows. Dim light filtered through a small glass brick in the wall, the only source of light in the cell.

I sat down. I had no idea if things had taken a turn for the better or the worse. I had been told that Germany was one of the best countries in the world. Therefore, nothing bad should happen to me here. It had to be better than living in war-stricken Sri Lanka. My initial ideas of Germany had been incorrect — no one had welcomed me with open arms at the airport. If the policemen hadn't arrested me, where would I have gone?

A few minutes later, another officer entered the cell.

"Stehen Sie auf! Ziehen Sie sich aus!"

Once again I pantomimed that I did not understand. He made gestures of stripping.

Hesitantly, I stood up and began undressing. A female officer then entered the room. Mortified, I did the best I could to hide my nakedness. She snapped on a pair of latex gloves.

"Gesicht zur Wand richten. Heben Sie Ihre beiden Arme hoch!" She indicated that I should face the wall and raise my arms.

The woman officer then kicked my ankles to force my legs apart, pinned me to the wall with her left arm, and inserted her right index and middle fingers into my rectum. I screamed in pain and struggled, but she pressed me harder into the wall even as I felt her fingers digging deeper and rutting about inside me. The pain was intense but the humiliation was blinding. All I could think about was the soldier on the train who had molested me.

I left my home for a better life and this is what happens?

She completed her exam and released me. I heard her snap off the gloves.

"Ziehen Sie Ihre Kleider wieder an."

I gathered from her gestures that I could put my clothes back on. The officers exited the cell, shutting the door and locking it.

Hours later, I was ordered out of my cell, and an officer took my fingerprints. I had not had anything to eat or drink for hours. I had no idea where my bag and passport were. Beginning a new life was not going to be nearly as easy as I had thought. I was ordered to follow yet another set of officers to another van. I climbed in without asking why. They climbed into the front of the van and we drove away.

In the van were two men: one looked Iranian and the other African. We did not speak or make eye contact. We kept our eyes on the ground. The van drove through a checkpoint, where we had our passports stamped with the mark of the Deutsche Demokratische Republik.

Welcome to West Berlin.

Of course, back then I did not know what West Berlin was.

The van turned into a small compound, which was heavily guarded by policemen. At the checkpoint, the driver showed the guard some papers, and then we got permission to enter the facility. Later, I realized that it was a refugee camp controlled by West Germany and the Allies who were in control of West Berlin: the United States, Britain, and France.

Tall iron gates stood at the front of the camp and high walls surrounded it. There was a guard by the front gate, and he and our driver exchanged words before the gate was buzzed open.

The driver drove the van inside the compound. Then a guard came out from the building and spoke to the officer in the van who eventually gave him my passport.

I saw the guard pass my passport to a processing officer of the camp. The processing officer looked briefly at me then turned away. *"Kommen Sie mit mir."*

The refugee centre was small, crowded, and completely enclosed. There were about one hundred detainees at the time. The centre was divided into separate sections or zones, each with about twenty bunk beds stacked in rows, one after another. As we walked through the centre, I noticed many of the men standing around were watching me with passive or hostile faces. The officer pointed at a bed. Then he left.

I sat down. The bed was reasonably comfortable, but I wasn't sure how I would ever sleep. I had never seen people of so many different nationalities before, and they were all very strange to me. They appeared angry and unfriendly.

A few minutes later, a bell rang, and the refugees all headed toward what I would soon learn was a cafeteria. As usual, I had no idea where I was headed but figured it made sense to follow the crowd.

The warm smell of cooking food immediately lifted my spirits. I was famished, and for a moment it hardly mattered that my arrival in Germany had been less than ideal. I lined up to get my food. The meal was pre-set and served on a tray. No plates.

There were tables with benches that lined the room. Groups of men sat together with their own kind and wolfed down their food. I got my food and sat on a bench. It reminded me of the boarding school dining room in Jaffna.

My first meal in my new home was completely foreign to me: roasted meat with peas, mashed potatoes, and gravy. The meat, I learned, was duck. I had never had duck before. It tasted like chicken! I managed to get off on the wrong foot during this first meal. In my family, we ate with our hands, so that is what I did. The meat was manageable, but the mashed potatoes and gravy proved a formidable challenge.

An older man across from me was watching me with a mixture of amusement and disappointment. He reached over and slapped down an unfamiliar utensil. I had noticed other men using this strange implement: a long, polished stem that spread into four sharp points. I picked it up.

"*Die Gabel!*" he barked gruffly around a mouthful of mashed potato.

"*Gabel?*" I repeated. The old man nodded.

Gabel, I thought. I did my best to imitate what I saw him doing. It was awkward at first — food kept falling off the fork — but after a while I caught the hang of it.

A fork, I thought. *What next?*

* * *

I was already familiar with living in a dorm from my school days in Jaffna. All I had to do was follow the rules and hope to get along with everyone.

I kept to myself as much as I could. I avoided people in general, and that included my fellow detainees. In the hall where I was staying, I met another Tamil. Once in a while I talked to him. He had arrived at the camp before me. He told me that people would stab each other with knives and forks stolen from the cafeteria. One night an argument broke out between two men — I think one was Iraqi and the other Iranian — and one of the men lost control and smashed the other in the face with his tray. In 1980, Iraqi forces had invaded Iran and there was a lot of hatred between Sunni and Shiite Muslims. It struck me that they had a lot in common with Tamils and Sinhalese. The guards rushed over and dragged the two men away. I never saw them again.

There was not much to do at night. Mostly we were ordered back to our sleeping areas, where we would sit for hours until lights out at 9:00 p.m. It was dull, but actually it was fine with me. I had no interest in fraternizing with the other men anyway.

Occasionally, I would hear loud screams, especially at night. Then, from my bed, I would see the flashing lights of ambulances and police cars shining through the windows. The vehicles would surround the camp, and there would be blood on the floor in the hallway the next day.

At regular intervals throughout the night, guards with flashlights checked each bed. I am not sure what they were looking for. Where did they think we could go? Maybe they were afraid of a detainee killing himself. At night, I was afraid to go to the bathroom; if I had to pee, I just held it in until morning, when the lights were turned back on.

Life in the camp was brutal and violent. Most of the fights were between Muslims, often between rival leftist and rightist factions of Iranians. Almost a quarter of the refugee camp was filled with Iranians. I wasn't sure what was going on outside the camp because we had no access to newspapers or radio or TV. In fact, I had no contact with anyone other than the Tamil man. It wasn't a place to make friends.

There was a lot of crime at the camp, too. Detainees would steal anything they could get their fingers on, and fights seemed to be a regular feature of camp life. I guess it was a way to relieve anger and frustration.

A short time after I was processed, I was told that the paperwork associated with asylum seekers took a month. I was so frightened and disoriented at the time that I really hadn't understood what that meant. Did that mean I *would* be granted asylum?

Every day I watched and waited. I never asked anyone else about it because I didn't want to cause trouble. I always smiled whenever I saw a guard, and I did as I was told.

I was at the camp for about three weeks. It is strange thinking back on it now. Were it not for the lights going on and off at regular intervals, I would have had no idea how much time was passing. As it was, it didn't seem to matter. It was like being trapped in a mindlessly dull time warp. I stared at the cement walls and tuned out.

Still, the bunk beds gave me a much better sense of security and comfort than the beach in Colombo. There was enough food to eat and a place to shower. I had no real complaints.

One morning a guard arrived at my sleeping area and told me to collect my things quickly. He led me to an office on the main floor. "What is happening?" I pleaded with my eyes. Over the last few weeks at the camp, I had not picked up even a smattering of German. The guards never talked to us, and everyone else at the camp was like me. When I arrived at the office, there was an officer standing behind the counter flipping though some documents. He finally looked at me.

"Loogaa ... Thaarrm ..." He was trying to pronounce my name but was unsuccessful.

I immediately nodded and acknowledged him.

He said something that sounded like "Nuremberg" and then presented my passport to another officer, who motioned me to follow him. He led me to the bus. There were about twenty people on the bus, a few of them women. I did not recognize anyone from the camp, so I assumed they must be from other camps. The bus left, and after a time we approached a checkpoint heavily guarded by soldiers. This, it turned out, was the border between West Berlin and East Germany.

The bus driver returned our passports to us and asked us to remain seated on the bus.

"*Halt Sie Ihre Pässe fest.*" Hold on to your passports.

Two border guards climbed onto the bus with a dog. One guard went to the back of the bus while the other checked in the front. They asked us for our passports and held each one up to each refugee's face, scrutinizing the features. All of a sudden, one guard ordered a refugee to get off the bus. His wife grabbed his hand and protested vehemently. The guards tugged at him, but she would not release her grip. Finally, one of the guards pushed her away and the man was dragged roughly off the bus. The woman was shouting and shrieking.

It scared the hell out of me. I watched from the window as they dragged the man into an office. His wife was weeping and shouting in Tamil something about him having shaved his moustache. I assumed she meant that was the reason he didn't look exactly like his passport picture. After he was led off, she had to stay on the bus with us. She sat down very slowly and went very quiet. It was like she was too scared to cry. I have no idea what happened to him.

There were a lot of soldiers with submachine guns. The situation reminded me of Sri Lanka, and there were certainly moments when I wondered if my decision to emigrate had been a foolish one.

The bus parked on top of a bridge that overlooked a nearly twelve-foot-tall concrete wall that stretched into the distance in both directions for as far as the eye could see. Later, of course, I would learn that this was the infamous Berlin Wall. Along the wall, I saw soldiers, holding submachine guns, stationed like dominoes, one after another, every twenty feet or so.

A guard stamped my passport "Drewitz," dated February 14, 1985, and returned it to me. Drewitz was known as Checkpoint Bravo on the German Democratic Republic side. It was the main checkpoint in and out of isolated Berlin before the wall came down. The guards decamped from the bus, the driver demanded our passports back, and we drove on into West Germany.

Later I learned that the border guards were allowed to carry guns and shoot illegal migrants. They were rewarded with medals and promotions for killing escapees. If the guards failed to shoot, or if there was suspicion that they had deliberately missed their targets, they were punished.

CHAPTER 17

After a long ride — about five hours — the bus finally reached a refugee compound in the city of Nuremberg. An officer at the refugee centre ordered us off the bus and instructed us to form a line for processing. Since there were only about twenty of us, processing took less than an hour. One by one we were ordered to step forward. When it was my turn, I walked inside the office, which was guarded by two or three men.

I was greeted in Tamil: "Vanakkam." The interpreter put his palms together in the traditional Tamil greeting.

"Vanakkam," I replied.

"What is your name and place of birth?" he asked.

"My name is Logathasan Tharmathurai. I was born in Jaffna, Sri Lanka."

He nodded and handed me a document. "Keep this with you at all times. Very important! Also, you must not leave Nuremberg. Do you understand?"

"Yes."

"You have an appointment scheduled that you must attend. Do you understand? Do not miss it. If you do, you will be in violation of the law and deported immediately."

I said I understood.

I was given a bus pass and about the equivalent of about ten U.S. dollars in Deutsch marks for pocket money.

An officer gave me a package wrapped in clear plastic. It contained a small pillow, a bed cover, and a thick wool blanket. He then led me to my room, which was located on the third floor. The room was freshly painted and immaculate. There was a wooden table with two chairs by the window and two beds opposite each other against the walls. One bed had clothes scattered over it. I put my bag and the package on the table and hopped onto the empty bed. I didn't even bother to make up my bed. It had been a long day. I closed my eyes.

For the first time in weeks, I was alone.

"Dinnertime! Let's go to the cafeteria."

The voice was yelling in Tamil, and when I opened my eyes, there was man in his late twenties standing over me: my roommate. At first, I was annoyed at being woken up, but then I realized I hadn't eaten anything for an entire day and was starving. I quickly got up and followed him out of the room.

"My name is Selvan," he told me. "I have been living here at the camp for almost two years."

"Really? You have been here for that long?" I was shocked. "My name is Logathasan, from Jaffna. I arrived today."

The cafeteria was big enough to seat about two hundred people. We waited in line and got our food: two slices of meat with gravy, a few pieces of boiled potatoes, and steamed vegetables, all neatly placed on a tray.

"This is horse meat," Selvan said.

I didn't care. I was hungry.

After dinner, I went back to my room and lay on my bed. My eyelids felt heavy and I couldn't keep my eyes open. I dozed off.

A loud noise woke me up. The sun's rays were penetrating the window. I must have slept for a long time. I had to pee badly, but there was no toilet in our room.

"The toilet is in the bathroom down the hallway," Selvan yelled in Tamil.

The bathrooms were communal, shared with other rooms. They were huge and accessible, with shower, bathtub, sink, and toilet. Everything was spotless and as modern as in a four-star hotel.

When I returned to our room, Selvan offered to show me the rest of the camp.

"This kitchen is shared by four rooms in our section. Keep it clean. On Mondays and Thursdays you can get food items from the main lobby, like whole chicken, rice, bread, and milk, to prepare your own meals."

I nodded.

"Write your name on anything you place in the fridge. Nobody will steal the food because it is already free. If the fridge is full, you can hang the chicken outside the window in our room. It is winter anyway." I assumed he was joking, but then I peeked through the window in the kitchen and saw a line of dead chickens hanging from ropes. "We are on the third floor," he said. "No animal can get them."

We headed back to our room.

"Nanri," I said. *Thank you.* At last, I felt genuine relief. My spirits lifted. Perhaps everything would work out after all!

Selvan gave me the address of the camp, and I sat down to write my first letter since I had left home two months earlier.

Dear Amma, Aiya, Kanna, Deicy, Jance, Vani, Kala, Sumathi and Sharmilee,

How are you? I am doing fine. I am staying in a camp in Germany. I have a nice room to sleep [in] and they give me food to eat. I am safe now and don't have to worry about being captured and tortured by the Sri Lankan army anymore.

I included fifty Deutsch marks [seventeen dollars U.S.] inside the carbon paper so that post office staff won't steal the money. That's all I have for now. Please spend it wisely. I will send you more money once I get a job.

Was Aiya able to open the Jewelry shop again? Is Kanna safe there? Tell Kanna don't go outside during curfews. You can write letters to this address:

Logathasan Tharmathurai
BAMF, 3rd Floor
Frankenstraße 210
90461 Nürnberg
West Germany

With love,
Rajan

As I was writing the letter, my heart sank to the ground. I felt immensely guilty for leaving my family in Sri Lanka. I had been able to escape the horrors of home, and I now had a place to sleep peacefully and eat three meals a day. But what about them?

Had the soldiers raided our village again? What was happening to my homeland? Why was there so much hatred among us? Why was war the solution?

I spent most of the time in my room doing nothing but sleeping. When I was younger, my mother would always say, "Rajan, you grow bigger during sleep. It is good for your brain," so I never felt bad if I overslept.

"Aiyoo ... Amma ..." I was moaning in my sleep as I dreamed about being chased by a military helicopter.

"Wake up, buddy, it is ten o'clock." Selvan was standing in front of my bed. I had slept for more than twelve hours. "Let's go outside and tour the city," he insisted.

I took a shower in the four-star washroom and then headed to the cafeteria for toast with jam and chocolate spread and a cup of tea.

After breakfast, Selvan and I left the camp on foot.

CHAPTER 18

In 1934, the city of Nuremberg hosted the infamous Nazi party rallies that were chronicled with incredible propagandist appeal by writer and director Leni Riefenstahl in *Triumph of the Will*. I came to know about the Nazis and Hitler while living at the Nuremberg camp. According to Selvan, the building we lived in had been used as a military hospital during the Second World War; after the war, the German government converted the hospital into a refugee camp. The history I learned was horrifying but familiar, too. The Nazis had murdered six million Jews. I wondered what the world thought about the genocide that was being perpetrated against the Tamils.

Selvan and I spent the whole day touring the city. Unlike my home village in Sri Lanka, Nuremberg was modern and clean. The roads seemed freshly paved and there were shiny new cars everywhere. Even the taxis were luxurious. Mercedes-Benzes! I was mesmerized by the traffic lights and by how polite and obedient people were while waiting to cross the street. When the lights turned green, they all started across; when the lights turned red, they all stopped!

It was still winter and snow covered the ground. I thought it looked so beautiful. Some older ladies wearing fur coats were walking their dogs on leashes along the sidewalk. Other ladies carried their dogs inside handbags. In Sri Lanka, the dogs roamed around the streets without any leash. Our beloved dog, Tony, was kept in our enclosed yard and never allowed to go out to the streets or come inside our home. In Germany, the dogs were very well taken care of and to me looked like rich, grumpy old men.

We went to a church nearby called Frauenkirche (Church of Our Lady). It took us less than an hour to get there on foot. The church and its adjacent buildings had been destroyed by the British during the war, but most of them had been restored back to their former glory. Inside the church, I was awed by the high ceilings and arches, the sculptures, and the stained-glass windows. Later I learned that this Gothic-style building was built between 1352 and 1362, under the orders of the Holy Roman Emperor Charles IV.

Every night, we were required to return to the refugee centre for meals and to sleep, but we were free to explore the city during the day. I started to go out by myself. I was particularly fascinated by the supermarkets. I had never seen so much stuff in my life. It was incredible.

One day when I was at the supermarket, a German lady flagged me down. She was holding a large paper bag that she indicated she wanted me to have. She smiled at me and said, "*Es ist ein Geschenk. Es ist kalt draußen.*"

When I opened the bag, I saw it was full of clothes. I smiled. There was a thick wool sweater and a heavy jacket. I thanked her as best I could for the generous gift and put on the sweater and jacket.

Most days I would hop on the bus and go for a short ride. All I had to do to ride the bus was show my pass. Of course, I was very careful to make sure I never travelled beyond the city limits. I had not forgotten the cavity search in East Berlin and had no reason to believe it would be any different in West Germany.

A month after my arrival, I appeared in the office at the detention centre for my appointment. The officer in charge greeted me with a smile and introduced me to a Tamil interpreter, who, I was told, would help explain the process I would go through in greater detail.

"Vanakkam." He put his palms together in the traditional Tamil greeting.

"Vanakkam," I replied. *Wonderful to meet you.*

The interpreter introduced himself. Then we all sat down, and the interpreter asked me to briefly summarize in writing my case for seeking asylum in Germany. I needed to convince the authorities that if I were to return to Sri Lanka, my life would be in immediate and direct danger. I obliged.

When I had finished, I handed my note to the interpreter, who read it aloud to the officer:

My name is Logathasan. I was born in Jaffna,
Sri Lanka. I am a student, and my mother
language is Tamil. The situation in Sri Lanka
is not safe for Tamils, especially for young
boys and men. If I stay in Sri Lanka, I will
be arrested by the military and will be killed.
I fear for my life. I would like to apply for
asylum.

The interpreter handed the note to the officer, who
stamped and filed the document. He also stamped my passport
— "12 March 1985 temporary refugee visa in Nuremberg,
West Germany" — and gave it to me. This was the first time
since I arrived in Berlin that I was able to keep my passport
with me.

"That is all for now," I was told.

The interpreter said that I would be required to come to
a follow-up appointment in one week. My passport received a
second stamp — "19 March 1985 Appointment for hearing in
Nuremberg, West Germany." I was reminded that I could not
leave Nuremberg. I said I understood.

I had a lot of free time while I was in Nuremberg. For some
reason, the older residents of the city were especially kind to
refugees, so I would go to the supermarkets and help the older
ladies carry their groceries. In return, they gave me tips. I saved
most of my allowance and tips and sent the money home to
my mother.

At the time, I didn't understand very much about Western
culture. I had no idea what a pub was. I'd never had a beer.
Occasionally, back home, my father would go to a rest house
in Jaffna to drink stouts with his friends, but I was always

told to stay in the car. The waiter would bring out sodas and chocolates for me. But as I walked past the bars and restaurants in Nuremberg, I could see patrons, singing and dancing, holding huge mugs filled with beer. I was curious but scared to go inside. The German people are much bigger and taller than I am. If a fight were to break out, I did not think I could handle the rowdiness. Occasionally I would go to the movies, although I didn't understand at all what was being said. After a while, though, I managed to pick up a few German words. *Danke.* Thank you. *Bitte.* Please. *Ja.* Yes. *Nein.* No. *Tut mir leid.* I am sorry. *Guten Morgen.* Good morning. But mostly I just said *Ich spreche kein Deutsch.* I don't speak German. Back at the camp, I learned some more colourful terms. *Arschloch.* Asshole. *Scheiße.* Shit. I didn't use those terms often. In any case, I found German very difficult to pronounce, so I doubt anyone would have understood me anyway.

I was very grateful to my German hosts. They were generous in helping thousands of refugees from all over the world. They gave us food and shelter and treated us with respect. My only surprise was learning from other Tamils at the camp that refugees were not allowed to work in Germany. Plus, qualifying for and obtaining permanent residency was not easy, and it could take many years. In addition to Selvan, I met several Tamils at the camp who had been living there for more than a year.

I was happy to be in Germany. It was so much better for me there than in Sri Lanka. From what I could understand from other Tamils, the war was not going well for the rebels. Had I stayed, I would have likely been arrested by then. Or even killed.

But I was not *accomplishing* anything in Germany. I wasn't happy about wasting months of my life riding buses around Nuremberg and helping old ladies with their groceries for tips.

I needed a real job. I needed to save enough money to bring my family out of Sri Lanka. I couldn't do that without a job. I was becoming very frustrated.

My mother wrote back to me. In her letter she included the phone number and address of my brother Lathy, who was still in France. It was the first news I had heard of Lathy since he had disappeared more than a year earlier.

France! *He must be doing well,* I thought. It was very exciting to hear that he was still there. I would contact him. I needed a plan for what to do next. Being in France, he would know what to do. Unfortunately, long-distance phone calls were very expensive at that time, and I had no money.

A Tamil man at the camp told me he knew a way to make long-distance phone calls for only five Deutsch marks ($1.70 U.S.), which was incredibly cheap. I agreed to try it and went with him to a phone booth. First, he dialed a long sequence of numbers from his head. Once cleared, he let me dial the phone number. "Are you sure this is okay?" I asked. I was paranoid about doing anything, even something minor, to jeopardize my status.

He assured me it was fine. I gave him the money.

Later I learned that the Tamil fellow was using stolen calling-card numbers to make calls. Apparently, this was a big business at the camp. He memorized the numbers so he wouldn't be caught with the cards. I am glad that I was so naive.

I managed to reach Lathy. He was thrilled to hear that I was in Germany. He said he would send someone to bring me to France so that I could stay with him. It was all set.

The truth is I should have been worried. I had been instructed, in no uncertain terms, more than once, that under no circumstances was I allowed to leave Nuremberg city limits. If I did, I'd been told, I would be deported back to Sri Lanka immediately. But here I was impulsively agreeing to leave Germany for France.

A week later, I received a note from a stranger at the camp. In the note, I was told to wait at the bus stop in front of the refugee camp the following day at 5:00 p.m.

I didn't tell anyone about my plan — not even Selvan.

The next day, I pretended that I was going for a walk and waited at the bus stop. To avoid attracting suspicion, I carried only my passport, the holy picture my mother had given me and some photos. No extra clothes. Nothing. Everything else I left behind.

At precisely the designated time, a Mercedes-Benz taxi pulled up; the driver instructed me to get in. He was German and seemed disinclined to chat. So I sat in the back seat and kept my mouth shut.

The scenery we passed after leaving the city was mostly forest and farmland. No towns or cities. We travelled for about three hours, and then the taxi dropped me off in front of a house in a wooded area that seemed, as far as I could tell, to be far away from any town. The driver turned his head and pointed to the house.

"*Gehen Sie hinein.*" I gathered I was supposed to go inside.

I had no money to pay the driver, and he must have sensed my hesitation because he made a gesture with both hands as if to say *It's taken care of.* I climbed out of the taxi, and he waved to me and drove away. It was dark, and somewhere around 8:00 p.m. I walked up to the house and knocked on the door.

The door opened, revealing a man who was clearly Sri Lankan. He nodded and smiled. "Vanakkam, ullai vango!" *Welcome, come inside!*

A woman holding a baby, presumably his wife, smiled at me. I smiled back.

"Have a seat here," the man said.

It was a very nice house, comfortable. A few minutes later, the man's wife brought me tea and biscuits. I had not realized how desperately hungry I was, and I made her laugh as I gobbled up the biscuits with both hands. The tea was delicious, and I thanked them. The woman disappeared with the baby, and I did not see her again. The man also excused himself, saying he had some affairs he needed to attend to. "You must be tired. Feel free to rest or sleep if you need to."

About two hours later, the husband came back into the room. "Your ride is here."

I said goodbye and thanked him for his generosity. He nodded. Another Mercedes-Benz taxi was waiting for me outside.

This time it was an older German lady driving, and she seemed more focused on her tasks. She was flipping through some papers. As soon as I got in, she drove off. For about half an hour we drove in complete silence along country roads in the dark. I saw nothing but trees on one side and nothing but trees on the other. For some reason, I assumed the taxi would take me to Paris, where Lathy lived. I figured Paris must be even bigger than Nuremberg. But when she finally stopped, we seemed to be in the middle of nowhere, at the side of the road at the bottom of a steep hill. The driver pointed. "*Auf diesen Hügel. Sie müssen gehen.*" It seemed she wanted me to walk up the hill.

I watched as the taillights of the taxi disappeared along the road. Suddenly it was pitch black. I could barely make out my hand in front of my face. It was also very cold. And quiet. I pulled my jacket tighter around me and began climbing.

The ground was blanketed in snow, even though it was early April. And the hill turned out to be more like a small but steep mountain. With no clear path, I found myself stumbling up the forested mountainside like a blind goat. I climbed for hours.

I was breathless and exhausted by the time I reached the crest. I was scratched and cut up from crashing through branches, bushes, and spiked brambles. And, frankly, I was grumpy and scared. Had my brother played a cruel joke on me? Had the second taxi driver stolen the fare and left me to die in some godforsaken nowhere? Just another dead refugee. After all, who would know to come looking for me? No one knew who I was or where I was supposed to be.

The moonlight shone very bright on the snow.

I was hungry and freezing. My breath drilled into the frigid darkness like puffs of smoke. I had to pee fiercely. But after a few minutes, once I had caught my breath, I actually felt rather elated at having conquered the mountain. Still, I had no idea where I was.

Suddenly, three people dressed in heavy coats emerged from the gloom. I realized they had been lurking behind the bushes. *This is it. They are here to kill me.*

"Hello! Don't be afraid. I am here to help you!" The voice spoke Tamil, and I breathed an enormous sigh of relief. The one who greeted me informed me that he was a guide who had instructions to lead me to safety.

"I don't understand," I said. "Where are we?"

"You are on the border between Germany and France."

The other two people introduced themselves. They were a husband and wife. Finally I realized what was happening. I was a Third World refugee with no visa to visit France, and if

I were caught outside Nuremberg, I would be deported. I was being smuggled into France.

"Let's go!" our guide said. "We don't have a lot of time."

The guide led us down the opposite side of the mountain. When we reached the bottom, he instructed us to hide in the bushes and wait.

I heard a strange howling. "Wolves," said the guide matter-of-factly.

They seemed very close.

"Do not worry," the young woman said. "They are not after you." She smiled reassuringly.

We waited about fifteen or twenty minutes; then out of the darkness about a hundred feet away came two blinking lights. They flashed three times, then stopped. Then again three flashing lights, then nothing.

"That's the signal." The guide told us to walk to the lights. "Good luck!" he said. Before I had a chance to thank him, he had disappeared.

The husband patted me on the shoulder. "Let's go."

We picked our way carefully toward the flashing lights. A car was parked beside a tree. A man who I assumed was the driver opened the back door and told us to get in. "You must hurry," he said. "And don't act suspicious."

All three of us jumped into the back seat and I closed the door. Within seconds, the car sped off. For the first time, I had a chance to have a conversation with my companions. The husband and wife were Tamils who were also escaping Sri Lanka in search of a better life. They said they had been staying at a camp in Hamburg.

"Here we go!" uttered the driver gravely. We were approaching a toll booth. "Hide yourselves!"

We crouched low, our heads between our knees. The car slowed enough for the driver to toss some coins into the bin, and as soon as the toll-booth light turned from red to green, he accelerated. It was thrilling. I felt like I was in a real-life James Bond movie.

After a while we settled in. The driver asked us in Tamil if we were from Sri Lanka.

We all replied, "Jaffna."

It was still dark outside. My feet were sopping wet. My toes felt as if they were frozen. I had my jacket on and suddenly felt very warm and exhausted. I could not keep my eyes open. After a while the driver stopped talking, and all I could hear was the sound of car tires on the wet road. I fell into a deep sleep. About five hours later, we arrived in Paris.

CHAPTER 19

My brother was living in a tiny apartment outside Paris with Suddy, our cousin who used to take us to the cinema, and two other guys. There were no proper beds, just two mattresses on the floor. During the day, we would prop the mattresses vertically against the wall so that we had space to move around. The washroom was tiny, perhaps a bit bigger than the average closet. The showerhead was directly above the toilet — a great way to save space, but it made it impossible to use both at the same time. The kitchen had a two-burner stove, a fridge, a sink, and a small table. There was no dining area, so we would sit on the floor in the living area to eat our meals. The owner had divided the tiny house into two apartments and rented both out. Another family was living next door. I doubt it was legal, but who would risk asking questions or making a complaint?

The apartment was located near the Saint-Maur Des Fossés commune, in the southeastern suburbs of the city. Our street was very quiet. There were mostly French people in the area and I did not see any Tamils. At the end of the street were a café and shop, which were busy in the mornings and evenings. During the summer, people would sit outside the café and sip espresso.

I had hoped that here in France, far away from home, Lathy and I might become close. But he didn't seem to have a lot of time for me. I was lonely for news of home. For family.

On the day I arrived, we talked about the family when we sat down to eat.

"Anna, eppadi sugam?" I asked. *Elder brother, how are you?*

"Nallai irukiran," he said with a smile. *I am fine.* "How is our father, mother, Kanna, Deicy, Jance, Vani, Kala, Sumathi, and Sharmilee?"

I told him how everyone was doing and that he was missed. I left the worst news for last. "The situation is bad in Sri Lanka," I said. "Our father is not doing well."

He nodded but did not say anything.

"Kanna is working at Indiran's jewellery shop. He is helping to feed the family now. It is not much, but it helps." Indiran is my uncle on my father's side. He also worked in the jewellery business, with the help of my father.

Lathy nodded again, only half-hearing me, and said, "Let's eat."

Once, Lathy brought home a fresh baguette for breakfast and made us tea. It was one of the nicest memories I have of my older brother. For the most part, though, he and I hardly spoke. If he wasn't busy at work — he and Suddy worked at a printing company — he was busy with his friends. On the weekends, he would go to visit friends by himself. He never invited me along.

One morning, not long after I arrived, he said I needed to go to the French immigration office with his friend Tasan. I was alarmed. I had no visa. I was in France illegally. Would I not be arrested?

"Do as I say. You will be fine," he told me. Then he left.

I accompanied Tasan to the immigration office. Tasan spoke to the officer in French. I have no idea what transpired, but the officer asked me for my passport and stamped it with a temporary visitor permit. Tasan told me to carry my passport with me at all times.

I was grateful that Lathy had done so much for me, but I do wonder whether he did it to get rid of me. Occasionally he gave me pocket money for expenses, and he would buy me a metro pass every month. Some days, I would take a bus from the apartment to the Saint-Maur–Créteil railway station, where I could catch a train in to Paris. The trip took roughly half an hour. From the top of the Arc de Triomphe, I would take in the view of the avenues and building spread symmetrically around the monument. The scale of the architecture took my breath away. I visited the Louvre and Napoleon's tomb, and I spent a lot of time at the Champ de Mars, a large public park next to the Eiffel Tower. Some nights, I would hang out on the historic Avenue des Champs-Élysées. I enjoyed wandering among the tourists along the cobblestone street and looking in the windows of the luxury shops. I loved to sample the street food, too. My favourite was a sandwich de Merguez: a fresh baguette with Dijon mustard, spicy ketchup, a grilled sausage, crispy french fries, and leeks. It was incredibly delicious and very cheap.

Policemen with drug-sniffing dogs were everywhere in the Paris metro stations. One day, a policeman approached me. *"Papiers!"* he demanded.

I handed him my passport, and after a few minutes of careful scrutiny, he handed it back and walked away. This happened often.

Occasionally, Tasan would go to the city with me. He and I took a lot of pictures of us standing next to the naked statues in the park. On the weekends, Suddy and I would often visit the Sacré-Cœur basilica. Walking on the streets near the basilica, we would watch the artists draw and paint.

I had learned to cook at the camp in Nuremberg, so on the nights I stayed home, I would make chicken curry and rice for dinner. During the day, our roommates and their friends would hang out in the apartment, and sometimes they brought over groceries and cooked a meal. Suddy knew them from back home, but I had never met them, as they were about five years older than me.

I lived in suburban Paris for about six months in 1985. During that time, I wrote letters to my family on a routine basis. Mother, of course, was happy that I was living with Lathy. I do not know if or how often Lathy wrote to her, but she answered my letters with letters to both of us. She told us the situation in Sri Lanka was getting worse. In May, seventy Tamil civilians were killed in what became known as the Valvettithurai massacre. The victims were reportedly rounded up by military forces and ordered to enter a library. A short time later, the library was blown up. In July, direct talks between Tamils and the government failed to bring any resolution to the civil war. It was very distressing news, but Lathy never wanted to talk about it.

Several times a week there would be a knock at the apartment door. I never recognized the people who came by; a couple were Caucasian, but most were Sri Lankan. Lathy never introduced them or explained to me who they were. If I asked, he would become angry and tell me to mind my own business.

It turned out that Lathy's roommate was a drug trafficker, and he hired people from the area to work for him. Lathy and Suddy never got involved because they were busy working at the printing company. Sometimes the drug-trafficking roommate and the people who came to the door would add white powder to shredded tobacco, then roll it up in a cigarette paper and smoke it. Other times they would put a little powder on a spoon and heat the bottom with a lighter. Once the powder was dissolved, they would use a hypodermic needle to inject the drug into their arms. It took effect very quickly. One minute they would be wide-eyed and animated, the next they would be on the floor, oblivious to the world, sometimes for hours. I would sit there, too, not knowing what to do. I'd had zero experience with drugs up to that point. A few times they asked me if I wanted to try it, but I said no.

If Lathy and Suddy came home and found the roommate and his associates in that state, they would become furious, so they only used drugs at the apartment while Lathy and Suddy were at work or out elsewhere. They were careful to put everything away before Lathy and Suddy returned home.

But they weren't just doing drugs themselves. The room-mate would bring home what looked like bricks of the white powder packed in sealed plastic bags. One of his friends would then run to the pharmacy to buy glucose. Using a credit card, they would make a mixture that was two parts powder, one part glucose, and package them into tiny plastic bags. Since I was often home and had nothing else to do, I would some-times help pack. We used a small balance to weigh the pow-der, five grams per bag. They never paid me, but I never asked for money.

One day, I was out with a Sri Lankan who had just arrived in Paris from Morocco two days earlier. His name was Pavan, and he was staying with us at the apartment. We were just walking around when, all of a sudden, he asked me if every-thing was okay. He seemed very nervous.

"Sure," I said. "Okay."

As we neared the train station, I noticed he had a locker key around his neck. We went into the station and I followed him to a locker. He took the key from the chain and very quickly opened the locker and yanked out a suitcase.

"Let's go!" He seemed in a hurry, and he was definitely agitated.

"Pavan, what's inside?"

"I will show you when we get home. Let's go." Clearly he wanted me to shut up.

My mind started to race. *Why did he leave the suitcase in the locker? Is there money inside? What if the police catch us? Am I going get caught along with him? Should I leave him and go in a different direction?* If I were to leave, he might not trust me anymore. He might tell the other roommate and his friends. It could affect our friendship. So I stayed with him.

Once we'd walked a few blocks, he calmed down a bit. Back at the apartment, he tossed the suitcase on the table and flipped it open. He dumped the clothes on the floor and used a small knife to pry up a panel from the bottom of the suitcase. It was filled with packets of white powder.

"You okay?" he asked with a practised smiled.

I nodded. "I'm fine." But I was terrified. My hands were shaking.

He emptied the packets into a large bag and weighed it on a scale. About two kilos.

Pavan continued living with us as a roommate. This kind of thing happened often, and before long I didn't think much about it. Lathy's roommates and I were hanging out all the time. Whenever I went out with them, they would pay. They even bought me new clothes. Money wasn't an issue.

Often, while we were packing up the powder, the room-mates and their friends would roll up a one-hundred franc note and snort the powder into their noses. They always seemed happy afterward. They would hug each other and sing Tamil songs. One day, curiosity got the better of me and I took a bit before mixing it with glucose, and I snorted it. At first, energy rushed through my entire body. I felt like I was floating in the air. Then my heart started to pound and I felt very hot and dizzy. I vomited. I became convinced that I was going to die. All I remember after that was sinking to the floor and lying down next to a pile of powder-filled bags. A few minutes later, I woke up with a terrible headache, my face wet. Pavan had slapped my cheeks and poured cold water on me to try to bring me around. That was the first and last time I tried cocaine.

I never saw either Lathy or Suddy taking drugs. It was like two separate worlds existed in our apartment. For the most part, everyone minded their own business. During the day, I often hung out with the drug-trafficking roommate and his friends. I suppose I was bored. What else was I supposed to do? I had no money. I could not speak French, could not work, and had no skills. Lathy was living his own life. The drug traffickers were Sri Lankans, so at least we had that in common.

One day our drug-trafficking roommate asked me to tag along with a white couple who were driving to downtown Paris in a white Mercedes-Benz. I couldn't imagine why, but I had nothing else to do. *Why not?* I thought. They dropped me off in front of a hotel; an hour later they returned to pick me up and we headed home. The white guy parked the car and told me to keep watch while he went to get something.

"Keep watch for what?" I asked.

"Just do it."

A few minutes later, he came back with a crowbar and wedged open the driver-side door casing. Inside were dozens of sealed bundles of cash. I pretended I hadn't seen anything.

Because I had a temporary visitor visa, I was allowed to attend a government-sponsored language school that had been set up for refugees. Classes were in the evenings, and not all the students attended the class regularly. The teacher didn't ask for any documents. Since I was Tamil, I am sure he assumed I was a refugee. The teacher, a native French speaker, spoke five other languages: Tamil, Hindi, German, English, and Spanish. I later found out that he was actually working as a spy for the French government. His mission was to infiltrate the immigrant drug-trafficking community within the area.

I spent about three months learning to read and speak French. Later, I found a job in Paris, working under the table. My boss was a distributer of model toys. I ran errands and did odd jobs for him, which included washing his black Jaguar, and I occasionally helped to assemble toys. I made about one hundred French francs (eleven U.S. dollars) a day.

He had a secretary named Katherine, who was from Korea. He and Katherine would often go to lunch and not come back to the store for two or three hours. When they did return, their hair and clothes would always be messed up. Though I was young and naive, I had a pretty clear idea what they were up to.

It was good to earn some extra cash, but I still wasn't getting any closer to my goal. I had the same problem in France that I had faced in Germany: I could not apply for a decent job because I didn't have my residency. I might as well have stayed in Germany.

One night at dinner, Suddy said, "Rajan, why don't you go to Canada and study there? You are wasting your life here."

"I don't know anybody in Canada," I replied. To be honest, at the time, I didn't even know where Canada was.

In Canada, Suddy told me, I could study for free and receive permanent residency in less than two years. Once I had that, he said, I could work freely and sponsor my family.

I was currently between a rock and a hard place. I couldn't go back to Germany; that option had died the moment I allowed myself to be smuggled into France. Besides, in Germany people like me were living as refugees for years. And at the time, unemployment was high in the country, so finding a well-paying job — especially for a foreigner — was unlikely. The chances of sponsoring my family to move to Germany were slim to none.

What about staying in France?

In addition to the problem of getting decent work, there was another reason I was thinking about leaving Paris. When I had first talked with Lathy, he had seemed very excited by the idea of my living with him. We could be brothers together! And for a while, I, too, had hopes that he and I could help to bring our family to Europe. That we could all be together as a family in France. It soon became obvious to me, however, that Lathy wanted me to leave. I wasn't sure that I could blame him. He had his residency already. He had a job. He had a life. *His* life. Plus, we had fought about my hanging out with the drug traffickers. I think, in his mind, being far away from home had relieved him of the burden of being the eldest son, the provider. But this meant that I had to be the one to get our family out of Sri Lanka. I had to do something!

Suddy told me he had a childhood friend who lived in Montreal. "You can stay with him," he suggested. He asked Lathy what he thought; Lathy said it was a great idea. He said he remembered Suddy's friend from Sri Lanka.

And that was that. The next day, Pavan took me to the metro station and I had my picture taken in a photo booth. We then waited at the station for a while, until we were approached by a man with one arm. He took the photos and told us to meet him at the same time in the same place the next day.

The next day, Pavan and I anxiously waited at the station. The one-armed man arrived with an envelope and gave it to Pavan, who gave him another envelope — I figured it contained cash. I don't know how much Pavan paid, but he told me it was all taken care of. I also don't know if Lathy gave him the money or if Pavan was being generous because I helped them with the drugs sometimes. He never asked me to pay him back, and I was broke anyway.

Back in the apartment, I opened the envelope to find a French passport. Below my picture was a very French name: Nicholas Bouchard. A semicircular government seal was stamped on my picture. At first, the thought of leaving Paris to travel to Canada scared me. But as the fear faded, I became excited about the possibility of a better future.

A couple of days later, Lathy, Suddy, and two of our room-mates drove me to Charles de Gaulle Airport. Lathy handed me a plane ticket along with my French passport. The destination printed on the ticket was Toronto, Canada. From there I would take another flight to Montreal where Suddy's friend lived.

I had left most of my belongings and my Sri Lankan passport with Lathy and carried only a small bag contain-ing some clothing. I said goodbye to everyone. I was sad to be leaving my brother. He still had Suddy, but I would be alone again. At the same time, I felt relief at the prospect of leaving Paris. Now I would be able to focus on my end goal, to rebuild the life that I had before and see my mother and siblings again. If I stayed in Paris, I would probably end up in prison for being involved with drugs. As I entered the airport, I reassured myself that, all things considered, it was better for me to leave.

On my way to the check-in counter, I was approached by a young man. He started to ask me questions in Tamil.

"Neenkal Tamila?" he asked. *Are you Tamil?*

"Oom. Unkada perr enna?" *Yes. What is your name?*

"Naan Ganesh. Unkada perr enna?" *I am Ganesh. What is your name?*

"Naan Logathasan." *I am Logathasan.*

"Enkai porial?" *Where are you going?*

"Canada," I said. "Neer?" *You?*

He smiled, beaming. "Canadavukku!" *To Canada.* "French theriuma?" *Do you know French?*

"Oom. Oru alavu therium." *Yes. I know a bit.*

He was from Sri Lanka, he explained, and he didn't speak French. I said I had to be going, apologized, and walked away. At the counter, I checked in and received my boarding pass. Having cleared security, I was walking to my gate when I heard my name being called from behind me.

"Logathasan, please help!"

I turned and saw one of the officers smack Ganesh with the palm of his hand.

Then three officers immediately surrounded me. One of them demanded to see my boarding pass and passport. I handed them over, and he grabbed me by the arm and ordered me to accompany him.

While I was being led away, I saw that Ganesh was surrounded by another group of police officers. He must have been caught using an illegal passport, and when he called for my help, the police guessed that I was also illegal.

I was led through a door and down a hall in the security section of the airport. In a small room, two officers instructed me to sit down, and they immediately began pummelling me with questions.

"Why did you turn back when the other man called out 'Logathasan'?"

"What is your real name?"

"Where are you from? You are not a French citizen."

If I were to tell them the truth, I knew, I would be deported back to Sri Lanka. I had no choice but to lie.

"My name is … Nicholas … Bouchard. I am from Paris, France."

I could tell, however, that they did not believe me. Their manner was very aggressive.

"You are going to prison. Do you understand that? You are going to prison!"

I gave up and confessed my name and my nationality.

"Stand up," the officer said. I was handcuffed and led to a holding cell inside the airport.

What a disaster! I was terrified. The cell was small, and like the one in Berlin, it had a sink, a toilet, and a cement sleeping bench cantilevered from the wall. I had no idea what time it was, but I figured it must have been late. I was given a blanket and told to go to sleep. I curled up on the bench and tried to rest, but all I could think about was how miserable I was, and how — once again — my dreams of a better life had suddenly been derailed. I was angry, too, that a kinsman — also once again — had betrayed me. I didn't eat or drink that night. I used the toilet in the cell to pee. It felt like the lowest point of my life.

This was it, I realized. This was where I was destined to be time and time again. I was home.

CHAPTER 20

Banging noises startled me awake. I rubbed my eyes and looked groggily around the room. My shoulders slumped in misery when I realized I had not been dreaming. I was in a cell and guards were banging on the bars.

"Let's have that blanket back."

A few minutes later a guard brought me a modest breakfast of orange juice, a baguette, and some cheese. I was immensely grateful and thanked him. Despite my despondent mood, the food was welcome. I ate as slowly as I could; somehow, being able to eat made my situation seem less dire. I finished the last crumbs of my baguette and waited. For what, I had no idea.

Perhaps an hour or so later, I was led out of the cell to have my fingerprints taken. Another few hours were occupied with filling out forms and being processed, none of which I understood. Then I was handcuffed and put into a van. Its windows were covered with wire mesh. There were five other prisoners inside the vehicle, all wearing handcuffs. They looked Arab or African. No one told us where we were going.

The drive lasted about two hours, but it felt like two days. No one spoke. Occasionally one of the men would look up and shake his head sadly. Everyone looked miserable. There is nothing more frightening than the look of complete defeat — the dead eyes of a man without hope, a man beyond redemption. I had no idea what lay in store for me. I didn't even know where we were. It was dark as we passed through what sounded like police checkpoints.

When the van finally came to a stop, the back door swung open and yet another faceless officer instructed us to step out. One by one, we filed out of the van and reassembled in a straight line for processing.

A guard removed my handcuffs and handed me a plastic bag and a folded grey inmate uniform. In a communal room, we disrobed and put on the prison uniforms. I put my clothes into the plastic bag and returned it to the guard.

"Follow me," he said.

Every ten steps we encountered a heavy metal door that had to be unlocked remotely. The guard would bark into his walkie-talkie, there would be a loud buzz, and the door would suddenly release.

I was led up a cement stairwell to the third floor. When we came to a hallway lined with a row of doors, the guard ordered me to stop. He barked into his walkie-talkie and a cell door coughed open. "Inside," he said. The door buzzed as it closed and locked behind me.

My new prison cell was more spacious than my brother's apartment in Paris and housed only two people. There was a bunk bed, a toilet, a sink, and even a small window. Photos of nude girls had been glued to the wall by the toilet and sink. The walls on three sides were cement; the fourth side had a door constructed of metal bars. The doors didn't have padlocks but deadbolts, operated remotely from the central guard station. There was a narrow opening near the foot of the door where a food tray could be slid in. The only light came from the window, also covered with iron bars, opposite the door.

When I entered the cell, an older man with a hangdog face was sitting on the top bunk, watching me. I nodded meekly. My plan was the same as always: have as little contact as possible with other detainees and hope for the best.

The bed had been made up with clean sheets and a pillow. Exhausted by my ordeal, I lay down right away and fell into a deep sleep. At one point I woke up to the sound of my cellmate sobbing. At first, I ignored his weeping and tried to fall back to sleep. This happened several times. I finally asked him, in primitive French, what the matter was.

He was from Mauritius, I managed to gather, and apparently he was very worried about his wife and children. I couldn't figure out exactly what the problem was and, in all honesty, I wasn't all that interested in finding out. He had a strange way about him, and he mumbled his words, barely articulate. I wasn't even sure he was aware I was in the room with him. After we talked, though, he seemed appeased and we both drifted off to sleep.

The next morning the guards woke us by banging on the bars. It seemed like an unnecessarily hostile method for waking someone. A guard demanded we slip our food tray through the opening in the bars.

We were given juice, grapes, cheese, and bread for breakfast. Lunch and dinner consisted of some variation of meat — slices of chicken or beef that often seemed as thin as paper — as well as peas and mashed potatoes. In the afternoons, we hung out in the courtyard. There was considerable diversity among the prisoners: Africans, Caucasians, Spaniards, Sri Lankans, and Arabs. Each tended to fraternize only with their own ethnic group, which gave them some security in case a fight broke out. Unlike the camps for immigrant detainees, this was a regular prison. My fellow inmates included drug smugglers, drug traffickers, murderers, thieves, and rapists.

Rouen Prison (also known as the Bonne-Nouvelle Prison) is located in the town of Rouen in the northwest Seine-Maritime district of France. Many years later, I learned that Rouen had been home to Nicolas Cocaign, the cannibal who killed a fellow prisoner and ate one of his lungs. Thankfully, this happened years after I was there.

Every evening, after our recreation time in the courtyard, we were instructed to go straight to the shower stalls. We would strip naked and put our dirty uniforms in a laundry bin. I knew it was common for prisoners to be molested or raped in the showers, so I would shower in less than sixty seconds. At just eighteen years old, I was the youngest person in the prison and thus a target. I was still haunted by memories of the molestation on the train. After showering, we were given clean uniforms and then ushered back to our cells.

Once a week, we were allowed to watch movies in a common room that could accommodate about one hundred inmates, who sat on long benches arranged in rows. The lights were kept on during the movies to deter the prisoners from fighting or partaking in any illicit behaviour.

I met a few of the other prisoners in the courtyard. One Sri Lankan Tamil prisoner told me that he had been incarcerated for four years for smuggling drugs. I immediately thought about my drug-dealing "friends" back in Paris. I guess I should have felt lucky.

It was depressing in prison, but the worst of it was not actually being incarcerated. What bothered me most was the unbearable waiting — not knowing what was happening from one minute to the next. Every hour seemed like an eternity. It felt like a lifetime ago that I had left Sri Lanka. I thought about Devi, and Nalini, and the kind Muslim woman who had taken me in. I thought about the nice old German lady who had given me a jacket. I thought about my mother and my family. What was happening to them? What did they imagine was happening to me? I doubt any of them pictured this.

I tried to keep to myself and not bring any attention to myself. I missed hearing Tamil, however, so I would talk to the other Tamil prisoner occasionally. He asked me what I had done. When I told him about my false French passport, he nodded. "Six months," he said authoritatively.

Six months!

"And then you will be sent back to Sri Lanka." He shook his head. "It is not good for a Tamil who has left Sri Lanka to be sent back by police."

I was devastated. What he said made sense. The government in Sri Lanka was anxious to get rid of Tamils. The news I had heard about the civil war was disturbing. Nothing was going well for the Tamils. If I was forced to return to Sri Lanka, I would likely be imprisoned — or worse. I felt desperately sick to my stomach.

Our prison cell window overlooked the yard, and I spent as much time as possible looking out, but there was nothing much to see. The prison complex was surrounded by high concrete walls topped by a metal mesh fence with barbed wire bunting. The wall was too high to see over. For all I knew, we could have been in a desert or on the moon. There were guards with rifles at the main entrance and on top of the buildings. I had heard from other prisoners that the prison was located in the middle of nowhere. There was nothing outside the walls and no people to be seen. If anyone tried to escape, I was warned, he would be shot by the guards.

"They wouldn't try and catch him? Bring him back?" I asked.

"Why? What is the point? Anyway, who would notice?"

No one tried to escape during my time there.

After being at Rouen for two weeks, I fell into a dark and hopeless despair. I would sit on my bed and gaze out the window for hours. I had no way of contacting my family. I had no news from home, no idea what was happening, and no idea what was to become of me. I felt deeply ashamed that I had promised my mother that I would make a better life for her and for our family. What had I accomplished? Nothing. Worse than nothing! Not only had I failed, I had now been branded a criminal.

I thought several times that suicide might be my best option. Now, I wonder if the only reason I didn't kill myself then was that I had no idea how to do it.

Late one night — it must have been around 9:00 p.m. — a guard appeared in front of my cell and rapped on the bars.

"Get up!" he said.

I had no idea what was going on and I pleaded for him to explain what was happening. But he just rapped the bars again with his baton and shouted at me. "Get up. Let's move it!"

When the door swung open, he turned me around and placed me in handcuffs. Now I was really scared.

"Follow me. Let's go."

He walked me down the hall and through the doors to the stairwell, then down to the first floor. He led me to another small cell. When the door was opened, he unlocked the handcuffs and ordered me inside. The door swung closed and I heard the lock click.

A few minutes later, another guard arrived. The door opened and he stepped in and handed me the plastic bag that contained my belongings. "Change your clothes," he said. "Put the prison clothes in the bin."

I still had no clue what was happening. *Am I being transferred to another prison? Am I being sent back to Sri Lanka?* Why was all this occurring at night? Nothing like this had happened before.

After changing clothes, I waited, wondering what was next. I was very tired, but my nerves were jumpy, itchy, as if electrified. As I waited in the holding cell, I watched as new inmates were brought in to begin a new stage in their miserable lives.

A few minutes later, the guard reappeared at the door. "Let's go."

I was led outside the prison to a van and instructed to get inside. We drove off, and about fifteen minutes later the van stopped and I was told to get out. We were at a railway station. I was baffled. The guard handed me a train ticket and said, "*Allez-vous-en!*" Go away!

I watched him walk away, not believing this could be happening. I waited in the darkness outside the train station as the van pulled away and drove off. It didn't come back. The night was deathly quiet.

I could not believe it. I was free! I had no idea how or why. *What just happened?* I wondered. *Why was I released?*

The station was empty at this hour. A clock on the wall indicated it was about 10:00 p.m. A few minutes later a train bound for Paris pulled into to the station and I climbed aboard. A couple of hours after that, I was back in Paris. It was now around midnight. I was too tired to walk and there was no bus or metro service close by, so I decided to splurge and use all the money I had on a cab. I hailed one, but when the driver told me the fare I realized I would be short. He would have to drop me halfway. I didn't mind. I was free!

It took about an hour or so to walk to my brother's apartment, but I was so happy that it seemed like no time at all. I rang the bell, and my brother opened the door.

"Okay. Here you are," he said matter-of-factly.

I was surprised at how calm he was. I told Lathy what had happened, but he seemed already to know. Suddy's friend had been waiting for me at the airport in Montreal. When I failed to show up, Lathy contacted an a French criminal lawyer. I am not sure how, but the lawyer managed to get me released. It made no sense to me, but I was too relieved to care. Only later did I realize that it must have cost a fortune.

It was a criminal offence to carry an illegal passport, a very serious offence in France. I could have been sent to prison for months or even years. I could not find the words to express the feeling of freedom I experienced. The moment I was released, everything felt so wonderful. Even the air smelled better! I was free from being attacked by fellow prisoners and from being told what to do next. I was able to wear my own clothes, eat whatever I wanted, and go anywhere I wished, whenever I wanted to. I was so grateful to my brother, and I felt ashamed about all the terrible things I had been thinking about him. He had acted like a true elder brother.

Lathy had saved me.

CHAPTER 21

I stayed at the apartment with Lathy, as before. When I asked him if I could work at the printing company with him, he said, "That will not be possible."

"Why not?" I asked.

He refused to even consider it and became very angry. "You should go to school and study!"

"I'm still struggling to learn French. How can I go to high school or university here?" I shouted back. I was so grateful for all that Lathy had done for me, but I was also angry: Lathy had a good job. If it was good enough for him, why not for me?

Later, I realized I was being unfair. Lathy had his own problems. And I was one of them. Everything I had done so far, starting with my big plan to escape Sri Lanka and make my fortune in Germany, I had done on impulse. And from the outset it had gone wrong. Looking back on it after all these years, I am amazed I made it as far as I did. It had been madness! Where would I have been without people like Devi or Nalini or the kind Muslim woman — or Lathy?

I resolved to spend as little time as possible at the apartment. For one thing, it was obvious that Lathy was even less enthusiastic about my being there than he had been the first time. For another, his roommates were still heavily involved in the drug-trafficking business and I was terrified I would be swept up in a raid and sent back to prison.

I had no real plan. I could not work in Paris — not legally, anyway. Escape to Canada now seemed off the table. And although my visitor visa had been extended, I had no idea what to do.

I had a Sri Lankan friend who was living in a refugee complex. I stayed with him for a few days at a time, avoiding the apartment. I hardly ever saw Lathy. I spent a lot of my time wandering around the city. The more I walked, the more I realized that I was going nowhere.

I knew little of what was happening back in Sri Lanka except for what I learned from my friend at the refugee complex. I never listened to the radio, and I had no access to Sri Lankan television news. Occasionally, I would find Tamil newspapers in my friend's room and read the headlines. But the civil war was on the other side of the world, and I felt hopeless and ashamed because I could not do anything about it or to help my family. I began to withdraw from news of Sri

Lanka and my attachment to my family. If I wrote without sending money, they would be disappointed. so I just stopped writing letters to them altogether.

After two months back in Paris, I was out of my mind with boredom. I had to try to leave France again. Suddy often talked about his friend Kris, who had gone to London, England, on a student visa to study. Apparently, England was the place to be. I decided to give it a try.

"You will be welcomed," Suddy told me.

"That's what I heard about Germany," I blurted out, feeling sorry for myself.

Lathy was insistent. "You cannot stay here and continue to do nothing."

He was right about that.

"It will be easier to get to England than Canada," he insisted. "You can learn English. That will be good. It will help you."

We all agreed: England was the best option.

Lathy spoke with one of our drug-trafficking roommates and arranged to purchase a fake French passport. After my recent arrest, I knew this action was several rungs up the ladder of criminal intent, and I felt very uneasy about it. But I convinced myself that I had no choice. I needed a new name and identity.

My new name would be — comically enough, in hindsight — Anthony François. My place of origin was Pondicherry, India; my nationality: French. In 1684, the French empire had colonized Pondicherry. It was a perfect match for my skin colour and my Indian background.

Since my fingerprints were on file with the French police, I arranged to travel to England via Amsterdam in the Netherlands. A few days later, Lathy, Suddy, and our drug-trafficking roommate drove me to Amsterdam. The drive was beautiful, and it felt more like a lovely holiday than a criminal escape. We stopped in Brussels, Belgium, then stayed in a hotel in Amsterdam for a couple of nights before my flight.

Suddy and I went for a stroll the night we arrived in Amsterdam. When we hit the city's red-light district, I looked around, my eyes wide with surprise. The narrow alleys were lined with bars and the streets glowed with red neon lights. Half-naked girls were displayed behind glass windows, waiting to be purchased for an hour or a night. The girls were very pretty, and they wore sexy lingerie and danced seductively and irresistibly. "They even take credit cards!" Suddy said with a smile.

I was too shocked and scared to do anything but window-shop.

I'm pretty sure Suddy was joking. I never saw him with these kinds of girls. At that time, I didn't really know what the girls would do for money, and I was afraid of catching a disease. And even if I had wanted to find out, Suddy wouldn't have let me. I wanted to have sex only with the girl I was going to marry. I resolved to stay focused on my ultimate goal.

Lathy purchased a plane ticket that would take me from Amsterdam to Dublin, Ireland.

"What is Ireland like?" I asked him.

"It doesn't matter," Lathy said. He told me Kris would meet me once I had arrived in Dublin. "That's all you need to know."

The next day, I said goodbye to Lathy once again and boarded the plane, this time with no issues. Travelling within Europe was much easier than going to Canada. At the airport, no one questioned me at the check-in counter or at immigration. It was a late flight, and there were no more than ten other passengers on the plane with me.

When the plane landed in Dublin, the officer on duty at the immigration counter was actually asleep. I couldn't believe it! I walked straight to the exit.

It was late September and the weather was cool and wet. I took a taxi into the city and asked the driver to drop me off at a bed and breakfast. There, an old man showed me to a modest but comfortable room. It had a bed and a small closet but no windows. There was a funny coin-operated heater next to the bed, and I woke up frequently during the night to pop in coins in order to stay warm.

The next day, I called Lathy and gave him my address in Dublin. A very young girl — she must have been the B & B owner's daughter — prepared breakfast for me: fried eggs, pork sausages, bacon, and toast. I found it unusual but delicious. She kept loading my plate with food.

I enjoyed walking around Dublin. I went to a movie theatre to see *A Nightmare on Elm Street* for the first time. Unable to understand the dialogue, I had little idea what was happening, but it made no difference. It was a horror movie and I loved it.

About a week after I arrived, I met up with Kris, Suddy's friend from England. He explained that we would be taking a ferry from Dublin to Liverpool. The next day, we checked out of the B & B and took a taxi to the Dublin port.

"Remember," Kris said, "do not talk to anyone."

I said I understood.

It was now early October, cold and damp. The huge body of water we were crossing reminded me a bit of the beaches in Jaffna, how the land just suddenly drops away, and beyond is nothing but water as far as the eye can see. I stood at the rail and gazed out across the water, thinking about my cell in Rouen Prison and the high walls that had surrounded it. Later, I would trace our route with my finger on a map. On the map it did not seem like a long way, but on the ferry, it felt like it took forever.

When we arrived at the terminal in Liverpool, immigration officers were conducting a random check of disembarking passengers. I stiffened when I saw them checking passports and IDs. I was convinced they were looking for me.

"Relax!" whispered Kris.

As the line inched closer and closer to the officers, my heart pounded harder and harder and my legs began to feel weak. My hands were sweating, even though it was so cold. It was Kris's turn. He handed the officer his passport. The officer asked him to step aside. *They are going to arrest him!* I thought.

Fortunately, his student visa was in order and he was waved through with no problem. I tried to remain calm, but my guts were churning. It was my turn. My legs were trembling; they felt as weak as rubber bands. I was convinced I would be asked for my passport. The officer would take one look at it and arrest me on the spot.

Anthony François? Seriously? Who the hell am I kidding?

The officer looked at me and nodded. I nodded back with a smile and walked past him to the exit. I felt as if I'd won a million dollars. I'd made it. I was free once again!

CHAPTER 22

After we got through immigration, Kris and I headed to a train station in Liverpool. We were both ecstatic. Kris admitted he had been flustered when he was pulled aside, even though he knew he had no cause for worry.

"You made it," he said.

I was so relieved I suddenly felt deflated, like an old balloon. I just had no emotion left. All I could do was smile and nod.

It was a long train ride to London, and I was very tired. But Kris wanted to talk. He asked me about Lathy and Suddy. We talked about my experience when I had been stopped by the police on my way to Canada. He told me he lived in a house in a neighbourhood called Wembley Park in London. The house, he said, was very close to the tube station.

About two and a half hours later, we arrived at the Euston railway station in London, then took the tube to Wembley Park. Kris and his brother rented the second floor of a home from a family who lived on the main floor. The flat was small but had a shared kitchen, a separate bathroom, and a bedroom. Kris used the bedroom, while his brother and I slept in the living room.

The neighbourhood was poor, but the rent was cheap. It also helped that the family who rented us the flat was from Sri Lanka. Having fellow Sri Lankans around made me feel less self-conscious and foolish for having left my home country in search of a better life. In fact, it was mostly Indians and Sri Lankans who lived in the area. A lot of the Indians owned grocery stores and mini-markets there, but I knew that wasn't something I wanted to do.

Every day I saw gangs of young people who looked just like me hanging out in front of the tube station, smoking cigarettes and shooting the breeze. I was determined to build a different life.

At that time, a person travelling in England on a French passport did not need a visa. But, since I had arrived in London illegally on a fake French passport, I couldn't apply for asylum. I would be arrested immediately. Therefore, I could not find any work legally.

So once again, I found myself stranded in a country that I could not call home. Had I learned nothing since I'd left home? It should have been obvious to me — especially after all this time and all I'd been through. It is hard for me to explain, hard for me to justify my complete naïveté during this time. I was not stupid. I knew the risks. But I had managed to convince myself to downplay them; the risks, I forced myself to believe, were nothing compared to the rewards to come. Perhaps I knew my dream of a better life for myself and my family was just that, a dream. But what else did I have left? What happens when you abandon a dream? Would I be better off without it? No. The dream was all I had.

I soon found a small private institution in the Wembley area that taught immigrants English. The tuition fee was almost five hundred pounds ($735 U.S.) for three months of lessons, an enormous sum for me at the time. I began working nights in a mini-market, paid in cash under the table. During the overnight shift, I emptied the fridges, wiped them with warm water, and then restocked them with jugs of milk, cheese, and eggs, putting the new items at the back and the older ones in the front. To this day, whenever I go to a supermarket, I always take my items from the back of the shelves.

I started my shift at the store around eleven at night and worked until about seven in the morning. I would then go to my English class straight from work.

Our instructor was a tall, thin Scottish woman with short hair. I had never met anyone from Scotland; I did not even know where Scotland was. She had a beautiful but strange accent. I had not realized there were so many different ways to speak English. She spoke very fast at the beginning, as if we were native English speakers, then she would stop and repeat what she had said very slowly. We spoke very slowly, too.

"Can you tell me how to get to Wembley Station?"

"Can …. you … tell me … how … to get … Wahmbley …"

She was an excellent teacher. At the end of the course, she gave us a test. She handed each of us a piece of paper with the lyrics of "Don't You Want Me?" on it, a song by the band The Human League. We had to listen to the song and fill in the missing lyrics.

She read off the first line of the song: "You were workin' as a waitress in a ..."

"Cocktail bar!"

"Correct. How about this one? 'I shook you up and ...'"

"Turning around!"

"*Turned you* around. Very good!"

She danced while playing the music. It was a fun way to learn.

After class, I was usually so tired that I would stagger home in the afternoon and sleep through the evening. I never felt comfortable with my situation, however. Every time I heard a knock at the door, I would seize up with panic, convinced that immigration officers had arrived to arrest me. In fact, Kris thought it very funny to bang on the door and shout "Open up!" It was not funny to me. It was awful. Kris had come to England to study at university and had no idea what it felt like to live as a fugitive.

Kris was very kind otherwise. He never asked me to pay rent, though I bought groceries occasionally, wanting to help out. I was sending most of my minimal pay back to my family in Sri Lanka. I also didn't know how to cook anything other than chicken curry, so Kris's brother would do the cooking most of the time.

I had been in London for six months. It had been fourteen months since I'd left Sri Lanka.

I was not satisfied with my life and was worried every single day. I had fled Sri Lanka determined to make my mark and start a new life, but what had I actually accomplished? My dream seemed further away than ever.

My illegal passport was due to expire in three months, and there was no chance it could be renewed, of course. And, in any case, I could not risk returning to Paris.

It was frustrating and depressing wanting to work and earn a decent amount of money but not having the opportunity. I wanted something more than just scraping by, living day to day, scared of every knock at the door. But most of all, I wanted my identity back. Although I had lived under my own name as a refugee in Germany and France, in England, I had assumed a false identity. But no matter who I was or who I pretended to be, I was still stuck and heading nowhere.

My instincts kept telling me that England was not the place for me to succeed and achieve my goals: to rebuild the life that I had before and to see my mother and siblings again. I had left my mother alone with my father, and I had no idea whether they were able to get enough food to feed my brother and sisters. I did not know if my family was safe in Sri Lanka, with the war, riots, and curfews. I felt guilty.

I thought, *If I don't try to leave now, I may get stuck in England forever. I may never see my mother again.* I kept analyzing the situation in my head. I had survived thus far, I told myself, so I had to give it another shot. I always regained my strength when I thought about my mother.

Without much real forethought — something that was becoming a habit — I decided my only remaining option was to try again to make it to Canada. I knew virtually nothing about Canada or why life should be any better there than anywhere else. After all, I had once been convinced Germany was the answer to all my problems! Still, I had learned from others that Canada was home to a large number of Tamil exiles. And from what I had been able to piece together, it sounded like a nice place.

A few days later, I booked a one-way ticket to Montreal. It was, I realize now, yet another rash and foolish action. But residing in England as an illegal immigrant for six months had been very stressful and I had to leave. As the date of my departure approached, I became increasingly anxious. The fear of getting caught and going to prison again was intolerable, and fear was my worst enemy. The day of my flight, Kris drove me out to London's Heathrow Airport and wished me all the best. I waited outside the terminal until the last possible minute, just before the airline closed the check-in counter. I had planned this so that the immigration officers wouldn't have enough time to ask me a lot of questions — or so I thought.

When I reached the counter, the agent scanned my passport, looked up at me, then turned and picked up a phone. I knew enough English by then to understand that she was talking to immigration; she wanted to verify my identity. She put the phone down, smiled, and asked me to wait just a minute. "It won't be long," she said pleasantly.

Very soon I saw from the corner of my eye an immigration officer walking quickly toward me. The two employees greeted each other and the agent handed over my passport. I did my best to remain calm.

The immigration officer flipped through my passport page by page, scrutinizing it carefully. At the same time, he asked me a series of questions.

"What is your name?"

I gave him my fake French name: Anthony François.

"Where are you going?"

"To Montreal."

"Why are you going to Montreal?"

As I was carrying a French passport, I figured my only recourse was to pretend I could not speak English. So, I pantomimed the gestures of not understanding what I was being asked. I then mumbled a few mangled phrases in my "native" French language — *Je ne parle pas anglais* and so on — and sighed with exasperation.

He looked at me. I could feel the heavy weight of doubt in his eyes.

I pretended to be confused. I sighed again, this time impatiently, hoping they might think I was a seasoned traveller upset about being delayed for no reason. I sighed as if to say, "I understand. You must do what you must!" I smiled.

The officer stared at me stonily. My smile collapsed.

"Wait here," he told me. He walked away with my passport.

The lounge was completely empty, and as the minutes ticked by, my resolve began to crumble. I could feel my heart rate quickening. The agent behind the counter had busied herself typing away at a screen, but I could feel her eyes on me, suspicious, perhaps worried I might at any second make a wild dash for freedom.

I waited as calmly and patiently as I could.

A few minutes later, a second officer appeared — a French-speaking officer.

"*Bonjour, monsieur!*"

My insides did a somersault. My French may have been marginally better than my English, but it was in no way good enough for me to pass for an authentic French citizen.

"*Comment allez-vous?*"

It was too late to play the mute card. I had blown that by speaking to the other officer. I had no choice but to blunder ahead.

I acted happily surprised. *"Bien! Et vous?"*

So far so good.

"Bien, merci. D'où êtes-vous?" he asked me. Where are you from?

"Je viens de Pondichéry, India."

I knew that if the officer went much further than this, I was sunk. The blood started to rush to my head, hammering at my temples, but I tried to maintain my composure, at least outwardly. Inside, I felt like a detonated building collapsing in a smoky heap of debris.

I smiled apologetically, hoping to appeal to his Gallic nationalism. "It is why my French is not very good," I said, in French.

He nodded, understanding.

Or, I thought suddenly, *does he already know I am lying and he's just playing along so I'll dig myself in deeper?*

He asked me the purpose of my visit to Canada.

"Montreal is a French colony, similar to where I am from. Therefore, I would like to travel there before I go back to India."

He wanted to call the French embassy to verify my passport; otherwise, he said, it would be quite impossible to issue a boarding pass. My passport was illegal — most likely it had been stolen. The theft had probably been reported and entered into a database. I was doomed once again.

I felt like a wounded animal, cornered by a much larger and more dangerous predator. I did what had come to seem normal to me. I kept lying.

"This is ridiculous!" I erupted suddenly, aping the mannerisms of an outraged innocent being unfairly harassed. "My friends in Montreal will be waiting for me! I am a French citizen who merely wants to visit a French-speaking city in Canada. This is very embarrassing!"

I noticed just a twinge of alarm in the officer's face. It was time to play my trump card. "Is this because I am Indian?" The issue of racial profiling was not nearly as sensitive then as it is today, but it seemed something in my manner had unnerved the officer. Or it might have been nothing. My French was not good and perhaps the officer had simply misunderstood me.

Apologetically, the officer assured me that my country of origin had nothing to do with this procedure. *Have no fear, sir.* He assured me, once again, that the questioning was purely routine, and that it would only be a matter of minutes, he was certain, before my passport was returned and the boarding pass issued.

I pretended to calm down and thanked him. "I understand. You are doing your job. I see."

A few minutes later, he came back and apologized. He explained again that he was only doing his job. "Your passport is in order, sir, and you are free to go. Happy travels!"

He authorized the counter agent to issue the boarding pass.

"I am sorry about the confusion," the agent apologized as she handed me my passport, ticket, and boarding pass.

"Fine," I said, shamelessly milking the role of offended traveller. "But I will have to think twice about flying with this airline again."

I wasn't sure how I'd gotten away with it, but I guessed that the real Anthony François had sold his passport, which is why he hadn't reported it stolen. I took the passport, ticket, and boarding pass and turned, briskly and in a bit of a huff, and walked quickly to security. Once through, I started running toward my departure gate. I heard my name over the loud speaker: "Last call for Montreal-bound passenger Anthony François! Gate forty-five!"

I kept running. Forty-eight … forty-seven … forty-six … Forty-five! I had made it!

I presented my boarding pass to the smiling agent at the gate.

"Monsieur François!" she said. "You just made it. We were about to leave without you!"

The officer beside her asked to see my passport. I told her it had just been reviewed. She was not impressed. "Your passport, sir."

She held the passport picture next to my face. I realized she was with Canadian immigration. A flight attendant closed the gate.

I couldn't believe it. I was so close! This could not be happening. Over the agent's walkie-talkie, I heard the pilot asking about the missing passenger. If I couldn't board now, they were going to leave without me.

"I need to be on that flight!" I told the officer urgently.

"Sir!" she said forcefully. "Step back. Stay calm."

She had more questions.

"What is your name?"

"Where are you going?"

"Why are you going to Montreal?"

"How long are you staying there?"

I answered each question in turn.

After what seemed an eternity, she appeared satisfied that all was in order.

"Sign the back of your boarding pass, please."

I had been practising the signature since I was in Paris, so it was a piece of cake. She looked at the signature on the boarding pass and compared it to the one in my passport. She nodded. "One last thing. Can I see your return flight ticket?"

My heart sank.

"You cannot travel without a return ticket, sir."

"I will be returning to India in a month, but I don't know the exact date."

She shook her head. "Without a return ticket, I cannot let you board the plane."

I felt hopeless but tried to mask my fear. I had only four hundred pounds ($588 U.S.) in my pocket. "Can I buy my return ticket now?" I asked. It was the only option I could think of. I hoped she would avoid the hassle and let me board instead. Surprisingly, she called the ticket counter, and they hand-delivered a return ticket. It was 360 pounds ($530 U.S.), non-refundable. The good news was that I was on my way to Montreal; the bad news was that I would be virtually destitute when I arrived.

Finally, the gate was reopened and I was allowed to board the plane. Naturally, as I made my way down the aisle, my fellow passengers were curious, and none too happy, to see who had been responsible for the long delay. I wondered — hoped — that many assumed I was an exotic celebrity. As soon as the aircraft doors closed, the plane taxied onto the runway. The flight was departing more than thirty minutes late.

I was spent, broke, and exhausted but happy. I had hurdled over a series of formidable obstacles. Not bad for a kid from a tiny village in Sri Lanka!

But my elation didn't last long. As soon as we were airborne and I was settled, my thoughts turned to dark imaginings of what awaited me in Montreal. *What if they find out that I have an illegal passport? What if the plane turns back to London in the middle of our flight?*

Settle down, I told myself. I was still worried that any second, armed officers would approach me and put me in handcuffs. My old roommate Pavan, who had vast experience in travelling, had once told me that if that ever happened, I should run to the bathroom and flush my passport down the toilet, then strip off all my clothes. "Immigration cannot remove you from a plane if you are naked," he assured me. It was, like most everything I had heard, complete and total rubbish. In any case, it was my Plan B.

I was ready.

CHAPTER 23

After many hours, the plane finally landed at Mirabel Airport in Montreal. I peered through the window and saw a scene similar to when I had arrived in East Berlin: everything was covered with snow.

Before I left London, my friends had told me that when I arrived I would have to surrender my illegal passport and declare my true identity to immigration officials at the airport so they would grant me asylum in Canada. It had to be done at the port of entry. If I were to leave the airport with the illegal passport and then try to apply for asylum, I would be deported back to Sri Lanka.

I was so nervous, torn between declaring my true identity and leaving the airport with an illegal identity as a French national and figuring it out later. I was tired of living as a fugitive, but what if I told them the truth and they arrested me and deported me anyway?

I sat on the plane and waited for everyone to leave. I was the last passenger to disembark and the last in line at immigration. Finally, it was my turn.

At the last moment, I decided to trust my instincts and take the risk. I approached the immigration officer and handed over my illegal passport. "I am Tamil from Sri Lanka and would like to apply for asylum here in Canada," I said.

I was not sure if the officer had heard me. My throat was so dry it was hard to speak. He did nothing at first, but finally he stood up from behind the desk and instructed me, with a flick of his hand, to follow him. We entered a small cinder-block office with no windows and just a few chairs. He motioned for me to sit down, then left and closed the door. I heard the click of a lock. I was alone.

I had gone through this situation so many times. Therefore, I once again trusted my instincts and suppressed my fears. I had nothing to lose, so I waited patiently. A few minutes later, the officer entered the room accompanied by a person carrying a tray loaded with food.

"Sir," the officer said, "welcome to Canada."

The other person put down the tray and left the room. I was confused. *This is for me?* The tray was filled with crackers, cheese, grapes, sandwiches, and soft drinks. It was more than enough to feed three people.

The officer sat down in front of me and explained that the paperwork would take awhile. "In the meantime, please enjoy these," he said and left the room.

Each time that I had been in this situation, the environment would have a sink, a toilet, and a cement bench cantilevered from the wall. This room was different. I did not feel threatened or like I was going to be cavity-searched as in Berlin. After the officer gave me an explanation, I felt safe and welcome. I was feeling more relaxed than ever before. Usually, I rushed to eat my meals to get it over with. But this time I enjoyed eating the food they provided. About an hour later, the officer returned with a Tamil interpreter and introduced us.

"Vanakkam, naan ummadai interpreter, Sivanathan." *Greetings, I am your interpreter, Sivanathan.*

He put his palms together. I did the same.

"Vanakkam," I replied.

"Ondukkum payappada vendam. Naan umakku uthavi seikirain." *Don't be afraid. I will help you.*

Sivanathan told me that I didn't have to worry anymore and he was there to help me to complete the paperwork. The officer would ask me series of questions, he said, which Sivanathan would translate into Tamil. Sivanathan would translate my answers into English, and the officer would take notes. When we were done with the questions, the officer gave me a blank piece of paper and asked me to write in Tamil a short statement for my refugee claim. Sivanathan told me not to say anything about living in other countries as a refugee. If I had already applied for asylum in another country, I would have to forfeit any claim for asylum in Canada. He said this in Tamil so the officer would not understand him. The statement was similar to what was written in Germany.

The officer took my statement and inserted it into his file along with my illegal passport. He then gave me what was called a refugee status claimant immigration paper. The interpreter explained to me that I would need to go to another immigration office in Montreal within a couple of weeks. The interpreter asked me if I had a place to stay.

"Yes, I am going to live with my friends here in Montreal," I replied. They noted the address in my file and then wished me all the best and told me I was free to leave.

Suddy had informed his friend about my flight details. When I exited the airport, Suddy's friend and his roommates were waiting for me outside. With a big smile on my face, I thanked them for meeting me. We went to their apartment.

My new roommates worked in factories and restaurants. After my follow-up meeting at the immigration office in Montreal, I was granted a temporary work permit. I got a job as a sandwich maker. I continued to remind myself of my ultimate goal: to rebuild the life that I had before and see my mother and siblings again.

I heard that Toronto had far greater job opportunities and higher wages than Montreal. My plan was to complete my education first and then get a decent job. I had learned French in France and English in London but decided to continue learning English, since I found it to be much easier than French; I would also need it to build my future. I kept thinking, *Should I stay in Montreal or move to Toronto for a couple of weeks?* Finally, I moved to Toronto.

I made the mistake of not finding a place to live before I moved — yet another impetuous decision. Once I'd arrived in Toronto, I called a friend of my Montreal roommate, and he allowed me to stay with him for a couple of weeks as I searched for another place to stay. I had only a small bag in my possession and was accustomed to sleeping on the floor, so frequent moves were no big deal. I lived in four different places in two months before settling in an apartment at King Street West and Dowling Avenue, in a neighbourhood called Parkdale. The apartment, which I shared with nine other guys, had one bedroom, a kitchen, a living room, and a bathroom. The rent was cheap when split between ten people. My share was only forty dollars (CAD) per month — what a steal! Five of the guys worked overnight shifts, so only five of us had to sleep in the bedroom at a time. Unlike in Paris, the mattresses were always set out on the floor for sleeping.

I found a job as a dishwasher at a restaurant in Mississauga. After my shift, I would hang out with the chef and waitresses. They would take me to the bars on the weekends; they drank beer while I had soda.

Now that I could hold a steady job, my first priority was to repay the loan to Prabhu's mother. Within two months, I had saved the twenty thousand rupees and paid back the money she had so generously lent to me. I continued sending money to my mother back home so that she was able to feed the family and keep them alive. Occasionally, I wrote her letters and sent her pictures to give her some sort of assurance that I was doing okay. She would write me back, and the thoughts and news of my family kept me going.

CHAPTER 24

When I moved to Toronto in May of 1986, the civil war in Sri Lanka was still raging. My mother and I exchanged letters frequently. Due to the war, it would take about a month for my letter to arrive in Sri Lanka and another month for me to receive one back. In the seventeen months or so since I'd left Sri Lanka, I hadn't received any letters from my father, nor had we spoken on the phone. But in June, soon after I moved to Toronto, I received a letter from my father dated May 9, 1986. I was still very angry with him, so I didn't open it. I did keep it, however.

In July, I received a telegram from my aunt, informing me that my father had been shot and killed by the Sri Lankan military.

Not long after I had arrived in Montreal, I learned that Lathy had left France and attempted to return to Sri Lanka. This had surprised me. He had actually made several attempts to return to Sri Lanka — he wanted to see our family and buy them a new home — but because of the war, he had been unsuccessful. So this time he had decided to try to enter from India.

When my father heard that Lathy was in India, he decided he had to see his eldest son. He arranged with the rebels to smuggle himself across the sea to India via a rebel outpost at Mannar Island, off the northwest coast of Sri Lanka. My father waited there all day, and when night fell, he boarded a small boat and headed across an open stretch of ocean about twenty-five miles wide to Rameswaram in Tamil Nadu, India.

Not long after its departure, the boat was spotted by the Sri Lankan Navy. The boat was ordered to halt, but the captain decided to try to outrun the authorities. The navy vessel opened fire on the boat, and the rebels fired back. More shots were fired. Clearly outgunned, the rebels hastily turned the boat around and roared back to Mannar Island. My father had been shot through the shoulder. When the boat reached shore, the captain and everyone else onboard jumped into the water and ran up the beach. My father, bleeding profusely, was too weak to run away. But he managed to make it to the beach, where he crawled into some deep bush.

The next morning, a priest who was walking along the beach found my father in the bush. The priest dragged my father to the church and hid him there. Medically, there was nothing he could do. The nearest hospital was many miles away and there was no way to get my father there without arousing the suspicion of the authorities. Most of the hospitals had been shut down due to a lack of staff and medical supplies. Some were destroyed in heavy bombing. A few days later, my uncle back home in Chavakachcheri received a note carried by the rebel underground: "Tharmathurai is injured by the navy and he is in Mannar."

My uncle wrote a message on the back: "Kanna, who is carrying this note, is his son. Please allow him to help his father."

It was up to my younger brother, Kanna, to travel to Mannar Island and find our father. He was only seventeen at the time and he was terrified. When Kanna found our father, he was in very bad shape. His wound had been wrapped up with a piece of cloth, but the bullet was still inside him. There was no hospital available to treat him. Kanna wanted to take him back to our village, but my father was stubborn. He insisted Kanna take him to India so that he could see Lathy.

How was Kanna supposed to get our wounded father to India by himself? My father had already tried and had been shot! But Kanna managed to make arrangements with the rebels to once again take a boat across the sea to India that night. He carried our half-dead father to the boat and helped him aboard. Miraculously, the boat reached Rameswaram without incident.

My father, however, had lost a lot of blood and there were no facilities in the area equipped to deal with a gunshot wound. The hospital staff said my brother would have to take him via ambulance to Ramanathapuram in Tamil Nadu, about an hour's drive away. On the way, my father fell unconscious and lapsed into a coma.

They managed to reach the hospital and Kanna stayed with our father there for seven days. A medical student named Nirmala would hide milk from her breakfast and give it to Kanna, as he had no money for food and nowhere to sleep. He slept by my father's feet the whole time. A week after arriving, my father died.

Kanna wrote a letter to Lathy informing him of our father's death, but the letter was returned: no such address.

It is customary in Hindu culture to cremate a body, but Kanna had no money for a cremation. Instead, he asked the hospital to bury my father in a paupers' cemetery near the hospital.

Kanna will not speak of this even to this day. Everyone in our village remembers my father as Chettiar Tharmathurai. *Chettiar* is a caste term that dates back ten thousand years in South India. It denotes a businessman of some achievement and distinction.

When I learned this news, I regretted that I had not talked to my father. And I thought of the letter I had received from him but refused to open because of my anger.

CHAPTER 25

I had completed grade ten in 1983 in Sri Lanka, but apart from the language classes I had attended in Europe, I had not been in school for about three years. I was now twenty years old, and although I was worried that I might fail the high-school assessment tests, I decided to give them a try. At Bloor Collegiate Institute in Toronto, I wrote tests for general math and for English as a second language, both in English. Studying English in England helped me comprehend the tests. The math was straightforward, mostly calculations, formulae, and some graphs.

A week later, I received a letter from Bloor Collegiate Institute informing me that I had been accepted into grade twelve. I was thrilled. The education was free for refugee students.

I started my schooling in September 1986. My first class was Grade 12 English Literature. Oh man, that was a tough one. I was baffled, and I didn't understand a thing. I left the classroom and went to see the counsellor. I asked him to transfer me to grade eleven because I couldn't keep up. My request was granted.

In 1986, the Canadian immigration system was clearing refugee backlogs and giving landed immigrant or permanent resident status to refugees who had come to Canada before the summer of 1986. I took advantage of that opportunity and applied for permanent residency while going to school and working. Within six months, I had gone for an interview and I received permanent resident status on April 10, 1987.

Things were finally moving in the right direction for me, and I decided it was time to sponsor my family to come to Canada. To sponsor my five immediate family members (my mother, three sisters, and brother), I had to prove that I had an income of at least thirty-one thousand dollars (CAD). At the time, I was making only seven dollars an hour working as a dishwasher and had just started high school. I didn't want to quit school just so that I could take another job to earn a higher income. Instead, I worked seventy hours a week at the restaurant and went to high school at the same time.

I would wake up at 7:00 a.m. and go to school. School ended at 3:30 p.m., and I would commute to work by 5:00 p.m. I did my homework during my commute. During the week, I would work eight-hour shifts and get home at about 2:00 a.m. On the weekends, I would work fifteen-hour shifts, starting at 10:00 a.m. and finishing at 1:00 a.m. the following morning. With overtime, I managed to meet the required income level — just barely — and sponsored

I received permanent resident status in Canada on April 10, 1987.

my family on October 5, 1987. It was one of the proudest moments of my life.

On school days, I skipped lunch and ate at night at the restaurant where I worked. The food was free, which helped me save money for my family's travel expenses. I would send money to my family back in Sri Lanka when I could.

As excited as I was that my family would eventually be joining me in Canada, I was exhausted. It wasn't easy working seventy hours a week and maintaining good grades at school. Whenever I felt low or was tempted to give up, which happened a lot, I reminded myself of what I had been through and what I had promised my mother and myself that I would accomplish. I was weak and tired, but thinking about the future made me stronger. Mentally, in fact, I was tougher than I had ever been, and the bouts of depression that had plagued me on and off for most of my life began to fade away.

One day, around three in the morning, I received a call from Sri Lanka. It was my mother. I was ecstatic to hear her voice after so many years. My mother, brother, and three sisters had arrived in Colombo for a medical checkup, a requirement for a Canadian visa.

We talked for about an hour before saying goodbye. She told me that the situation in Sri Lanka had deteriorated badly. Chavakachcheri had become a ghost town. Most of the buildings had been damaged by bombs, and bullet holes could be seen on the walls and doors everywhere. The once-popular market was empty. No one walked the streets. My mother said she would visit neighbours at home and buy vegetables from them. It was not safe being outdoors.

She said young boys and men who had been shot by the army were hung upside down from trees along the streets as a warning to others. Sometimes they were still alive when they were hung upside down with their hands tied behind their back. Dogs would gather in hungry packs under the bodies to lick up the puddles of blood in the street.

Whenever they heard the army trucks on the road, my mother told me, she and my sisters would hide inside a bunker in the backyard of our house. One night they stayed in the bunker all night, surrounded by complete darkness. They were terrified of leaving for even a second. She said that during the night they heard screams coming from a neighbouring house. Fighting then broke out among the soldiers, followed by silence.

The next morning, they crawled out, tired, hungry, and thirsty but unharmed. When my mother went next door, she discovered the neighbour's young daughters had been raped and murdered by a gang of soldiers. It could so easily have been them.

Two months later, I received another phone call from my mother. She had good news: their Canadian visas had been approved.

They were coming home. To a new and better home.

Monday, July 25, 1988, was one of the happiest days of my life. I had been waiting for this moment for more than three years. That day, one of my work colleagues drove me to the Toronto airport, where we waited for my family's arrival. First, I spotted my mother walking with my sisters Jance and Vani, holding their hands. Then I saw Kanna and Deicy following behind them, carrying the luggage. I ran to my mother and hugged her. Emotions welled up inside everyone, and we all started to cry. It had been so long since we had seen one another, and it felt so right to be together again. We were all overwhelmed with joy as we left the airport.

In anticipation of their arrival, I had rented a one-bedroom apartment in Scarborough. Most of my earnings went to pay the rent, so I had very little money left over to feed the six of us. Since I had sponsored my family, we couldn't seek help from the government. Because we couldn't afford to buy beds, we slept with comforters on the floor. My mother and sisters slept in the bedroom, and Kanna and I slept in the living room. I bought a dining table and four chairs from the Salvation Army store — three subway trips saved the delivery fees. We went to a Goodwill store and picked up some clothes to keep us warm during the winter.

Half a year later, my mother and my brother found jobs in a factory, which helped to cover the expenses. My sisters, aged twelve, sixteen, and eighteen, were going to school. During the day, I worked as a computer operator for a company in Scarborough, and at night I went to Centennial College to study computer programming. Slowly, life started to get better and better, day by day. I no longer had to worry about my family getting killed back home, nor about living as a fugitive. I began to forget the past and started looking forward to the future.

CHAPTER 26

A lthough my family was safe now in Canada, it was still hard for me to accept the fact that my father was dead. Many months after he was murdered, I finally brought myself to open his letter. The case he refers to in the letter involved Lathy. When my brother travelled to India from France, he carried with him a rather large sum of money, which was seized by customs officials at the airport. In order to have the money returned, Lathy was required to petition the court.

9-5-86

Dear son Rajan:

Your dear Aiya [father] is fine. I am curious about you?

Amma [mother], Kanna, Deicy, Kala, Jance, Vani, Sumathi, and Sharmilee are very fine.

Anna [Lathy] is in Madras [India] and sends some things via Pappa [Suddy's younger brother]: two sarees, five dresses and other things.

Once his case is over, they will return the money. He may come here otherwise he may go back to France. I prayed to the goddess Sri Meenakshi Amman. Once he wins, I promised to do the Abhishekam to goddess Sri Meenakshi Amman [Hindu ritual of thanks].

If Anna comes back, the lenders will be after us. Therefore, he needs to live here secretly.

Pappa came here on a boat. I lost my identity card. Without having a job, I am going crazy at home. Ask Indiran uncle [father's brother] to open a shop for me. He is delaying it. I believe he refuses to help me. Perhaps, if Anna comes here, I am hoping to open a shop. Otherwise, I am going to go outside the country.

Here I am doing nothing and fighting with your mother. Everyone is teasing me now that I don't have a business.

Write me about how are you doing? Don't worry about us. You should live happily. You should watch your body [health] — remember, you need a wall to draw a picture [a familiar Tamil expression]. It is in your hands for us to gain back the good status.

I wrote to Anna to not buy a house or land here now — maybe after two or three years, then it may be okay to buy. Study carefully. Don't take baths in the sea [at my birth it was prophesied that I would die in water]. We are worried about both of you all the time. Bad things happened to Anna's hard-earned money. However, I strongly believe he will get it back.

Anna sent 100 dollars. I am going to use some of it to buy a cycle. When did you send your last letter? Did you send any money? I didn't get any. If you send letters to Indiran's shop, I will never get them. Therefore, send letters to our home address. I never received any letters since you sent the birthday card. After January along with 300 dollars, I never received any money. If you sent any, write a letter. If you have money, send it to me. I am going to talk to Anna via a telephone soon. Write me letters. Don't forget. Also write to me how much money you sent it and when did you sent it.

Loving Aiya,
C.R. Tharmathurai

9-5-86

Last letter (written in Tamil) that I received from my father, dated May 9, 1986, before he died on July 1, 1986.

I felt horribly guilty, of course, and furious — unappeasably so. And I gripped my anger like a lifeline.

It took many years for my anger to diminish — not just anger at my father but at the world at large. I have now let go of it. I have learned to forgive others' mistakes and to understand what love is. When we die, we bring nothing with us. We leave only our legacy behind to remind others how we lived.

We don't get to choose our fathers. We must all make do.

I read my father's letter again recently and cried. Not for me but for my father. For what he tried and failed to be.

At the same time that Kanna and my father had gone to India to find Lathy, Lathy was able to get his money back from Indian customs and travel to Sri Lanka with help from the rebels. When he returned home, he bought a house in Chavakachcheri for our family and helped them get settled there. My father had written a letter to my aunt when he left for India. She, Sumathi, and Sharmilee came back and lived with Lathy, my mother, and my siblings in Chavakachcheri. Two months later, Lathy was shot in the leg by the Sri Lankan Army and was hospitalized for many months.

My mother and the rest of my siblings lived with Lathy for two years and then left for Canada in July 1988. Lathy continued to live with our aunt and our half-sisters in Chavakachcheri. After my mother got her job in the factory in Scarborough, she was able to sponsor Lathy into Canada, even though he was an adult, because he was her only child left behind in Sri Lanka.

Lathy finally came to Toronto in 1989 and was reunited with our family. Our aunt and half-sisters remained living in the house that Lathy had bought in Chavakachcheri. Over time, my brothers and sisters got married and moved on with their lives. My mother continues to live with me to this very day.

EPILOGUE

Desire is the key to motivation, but it's the determination
and commitment to unrelenting pursuit of your goal —
a commitment to excellence — that will enable you
to attain the success you seek.
— Mario Andretti, Italian American
world-champion race-car driver

I have kept my memories alive by reviewing them mentally, even reliving some of the worst memories in
my dreams. The haunting fears of getting arrested,
molested, or killed by the military; being robbed and killed
by the mobs in Colombo; being cheated by other Tamils;
getting attacked in the prison; and getting deported back to

Sri Lanka were all things that I suffered with privately, that I kept locked up inside me for the majority of my life. Writing this memoir was my first step toward effectively dealing with this trauma, and I feel it has contributed to making me a stronger person overall.

Despite my past and the struggles I have faced, I have been very fortunate to build a career in information systems at a Fortune 500 company. My colleagues have often asked me about what I went through in Sri Lanka, and I have shared the story about being chased by a military helicopter. I am sure that I suffered from post-traumatic stress disorder, and I can understand how many veterans feel after experiencing war.

For many years, I was deeply ashamed by the incident with the soldiers on the train, and it wasn't until recently, at the age of fifty, that I finally shared the story of this experience with my wife. She was the first person to know that I had been molested and has been very supportive, especially when I expressed how I felt.

My wife is the love of my life, and I met her here in Canada. We have been married for almost thirty years now and have been blessed with two wonderful boys, Eric and Daniel. Both have completed their university studies and are trying to make their own dreams come true.

I have been given so many extraordinary opportunities in Canada that I could never have imagined. I am so grateful to this country for the warm welcome I received.

I remember when I was twelve years old, my father took me with him to visit a friend of his. As he introduced me, he told his friend that his son was "brilliant" and that "he will be very successful one day."

I have been living in Canada now for more than three decades. I have a wonderful family, and I got the education I had always wanted. Although my father is long dead, I still wanted to prove to him that he was right. I wanted him to be proud.

I think he would be.

ACKNOWLEDGEMENTS

When I described some of the challenges that I had faced in my life to my friends, they encouraged me to share my story with the world. My painful experiences have been burning inside of me for more than thirty years, but now I've been able to get them out of my system. Thank you, dear reader, for taking the time to read my story.

I would like to express my sincere thanks to my mother, who never lost hope while going through the many ups and downs in her life. She was able to protect our family and keep everyone alive through civil war and poverty.

I would like to thank my love, Celia, who lost both of her parents when she was young, lived as an orphan, and took care of her younger brother. She accepted me for who I am.

Thank you, Robin Ramesra and Teresa Ward for encouraging me to write my story.

Greg Ioannou, I am grateful for your mentorship. You have an amazing team that provided me with invaluable support.

Finally, special thanks Elham Ali, Laura Boyle, Carl Brand, Crissy Calhoun, Susan Fitzgerald, Rudi Garcia, Allison Hirst, Kirk Howard, Kathryn Lane, Heather McLeod, Elena Radic, Rachel Spence, and others from Dundurn Press for their tremendous support and guidance to share my story with the world.

Book Credits

Acquiring Editor: Kathryn Lane
Developmental Editor: Allison Hirst
Project Editor: Elena Radic
Editorial Assistant: Melissa Kawaguchi
Copy Editor: Susan Fitzgerald
Proofreader: Crissy Calhoun

Designer: Laura Boyle

Publicist: Elham Ali

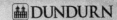